Architectural Design
March/April 2006

Techniques and Technologies
in Morphogenetic Design

Guest-edited by
Michael Hensel, Achim Menges + Michael Weinstock

D0557897

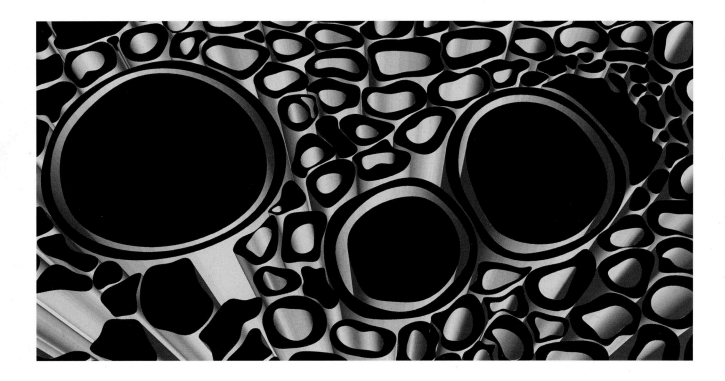

🕊 WILEY-ACADEMY

ISBN-13 9780470015292
ISBN-10 0470015292
Profile No 180
Vol 76 No 2

12

Editorial Offices
International House
Ealing Broadway Centre
London W5 5DB

T: +44 (0)20 8326 3800
F: +44 (0)20 8326 3801
E: architecturaldesign@wiley.co.uk

Editor
Helen Castle

Design and Editorial Management
Mariangela Palazzi-Williams

Art Direction/Design
Christian Küsters (CHK Design)

Design
Hannah Dumphy (CHK Design)

Project Coordinator and Picture Editor
Caroline Ellerby

Advertisement Sales
Faith Pidduck/Wayne Frost
T +44 (0)1243 770254
E fpidduck@wiley.co.uk

Editorial Board
Will Alsop, Denise Bratton, Adriaan Beukers,
André Chaszar, Peter Cook, Teddy Cruz,
Max Fordham, Massimiliano Fuksas,
Edwin Heathcote, Anthony Hunt,
Charles Jencks, Jan Kaplicky, Robert Maxwell,
Jayne Merkel, Monica Pidgeon,
Antoine Predock, Michael Rotondi,
Leon van Schaik, Ken Yeang

Contributing Editors
André Chaszar
Jeremy Melvin
Jayne Merkel

Abbreviated positions
b = bottom, c = centre, l = left, r = right

Front cover: Plan view of the differentiated lattice system derived through a morphogenetic design technique for OCEAN NORTH's Jyväskylä Music and Art Centre © OCEAN NORTH

_AD_
p 5 © Gusto/Science Photo Library; pp 6 & 76-77 © Finnforest Merk; pp 7, 10, 62 & 68-69 © OCEAN NORTH; pp 8 & 80-81, 82(t&b), 83, 84(tl&bl), 85(br), 85(t), 86-89, 93-95 © Achim Menges; p 9 © Michael Hensel & Achim Menges/David Newton & Joe Kellner; p 12 © Science Photo Library; pp 14, 20, 36(r) © Eye of Science/Science Photo Library; p 15 © Philippe Psaila/Science Photo Library; pp 16-17, 24 © Michael Hensel; p 18 © National Institutes of Health/Science Photo Library; p 21(t) © Alexis Rosenfeld/Science Photo Library; p 21(b) © Pascal Goetgheluck/Science Photo Library; p 22 © Outlast Technologies/Science Photo Library; p 23 © Sam Ogden/Science Photo Library; pp 26-33, 37(r), 54, 55(l), 57 © Michael Weinstock; p 34 © Sasumu Nishinaga/Science Photo Library; p 36(l) © Dr Jeremy Burgess/Science Photo Library; p 37(l) © Steve Gschmeissner/Science Photo Library; p 38 © Arup; pp 39-41 © CSCEC + PTW + Arup; pp 42 & 48-49 © Foster and Partners; p 47 © Robert Aish/Bentley Systems; pp 50-53 © Kohn Pederson Fox Associates (International); pp 55(r) & 56 © Arup; pp 60, 64(r&bl) & 65 © Daniel Coll I Capdevila; pp 66-67 © Neri Oxman; p 64(tl) © Michael Hensel/Achim Menges; pp 70 & 74 © Stadion GmbH – München, photos B Ducke; pp 71-72 © Octatube Space Structures; p 73 © Skyspan (Europe) GmbH; p 75 © Seele UK; pp 78 & 82(c) © Achim Menges, photos Chad Loucks; p 84(tr) © Francis Ware; p 84(br) © Andrew Kudless; p 85(bl) © Sue Barr; pp 90-91 © Mattia Gambardella & Giannis Douridas; p 92 © Pavel Hladik.

_AD+_
pp 98-99, 100(r) & 101(c&r)© Timothy Hursley/MoMA; p 100(tl) © Union Square Hospitality, photo Quentin Bacon; p 101(l) courtesy of the Museum of Modern Art; pp 102-103 & 105(b) © Nick Kane; pp 104, 105(tl&r) © Niall McLaughlin Architects; pp 106 & 108-111 © Urban Projects, photos Ciaran O'Brian; p 107 © Urban Projects, photo Derek Tynan ; pp 112 & 121 © Filippo Romano; pp 116-117, 120(l) © Filippo Fortis; pp 118-119, 120(c&r) © Metrogramma; p 122 © Will McLean; p 123 courtesy Sir Harry Kroto; p 124 © Leon van Schaik; pp 125 & 127 © Peter Bennetts; p 126 © Minifie Nixon.

Published in Great Britain in 2006 by Wiley-Academy, a division of John Wiley & Sons Ltd Copyright © 2006, John Wiley & Sons Ltd, The Atrium, Southern Gate, Chichester, West Sussex PO19 8SQ, England, Telephone +44 (0)1243 779777
Email (for orders and customer service enquiries): cs-books@wiley.co.uk
Visit our Home Page on wileyeurope.com or wiley.com

Requests to the Publisher should be addressed to:
Permissions Department,
John Wiley & Sons Ltd,
The Atrium
Southern Gate
Chichester,
West Sussex PO19 8SQ
England

F: +44 (0)1243 770571
E: permreq@wiley.co.uk

Subscription Offices UK
John Wiley & Sons Ltd
Journals Administration Department
1 Oldlands Way, Bognor Regis
West Sussex, PO22 9SA
T: +44 (0)1243 843272
F: +44 (0)1243 843232
E: cs-journals@wiley.co.uk

Printed in Italy by Conti Tipicolor.
All prices are subject to change without notice.
[ISSN: 0003-8504]
Reprinted June 2011

_AD_ is published bimonthly and is available to purchase on both a subscription basis and as individual volumes at the following prices.

Single Issues
Single issues UK: £22.99
Single issues outside UK: US$45.00
Details of postage and packing charges available on request.

Annual Subscription Rates 2005
Institutional Rate
Print only or Online only: UK£175/US$290
Combined Print and Online:
UK£193/US$320
Personal Rate
Print only: UK£99/US$155
Student Rate
Print only: UK£70/US$110

Prices are for six issues and include postage and handling charges. Periodicals postage paid at Jamaica, NY 11431. Air freight and mailing in the USA by Publications Expediting Services Inc, 200 Meacham Avenue, Elmont, NY 11003

Individual rate subscriptions must be paid by personal cheque or credit card. Individual rate subscriptions may not be resold or used as library copies.

Postmaster
Send address changes to 3 Publications Expediting Services, 200 Meacham Avenue, Elmont, NY 11003

Contents

70

54

Editorial

The cover title of this issue, *Techniques and Technologies in Morphogenetic Design*, provides it with a very wide frame: morphogenesis pertains not only to the development of form and structure in an organism, but also to an organism's evolutionary development over time. It is, in effect, a substantial signpost that in a broad brushstroke takes in the whole gamut of natural systems, both current and in evolution. It is indicative of the not inconsiderable, some might say infinite, project that guest-editors Michael Hensel, Achim Menges and Michael Weinstock have taken on through their activities in the Emergence and Design Group and their teaching and research at the Architectural Association (aa) in London. By studying the complex and dynamic exchange between organisms and their environment, they have sought out a new model for architecture – one that through the application of biochemical processes and the functionality of life is in empathy rather than at odds with natural ecology. By keeping their eye on this higher goal, the group is providing a prescient new ecological paradigm for architecture that seeks, through new scientific advances in the visualisation and understanding of natural processes and systems, to leave behind the known structural and material building blocks of architecture.

What the generic quality of the 'morphogenetic design' tag belies is the specificity and focus that Hensel, Menges and Weinstock have brought to their subject in this volume. This issue is the sequel to *D Emergence: Morphogenetic Design Strategies*, published two years ago. It is, however, no Emergence II. Whereas in the first issue, the potential of the project was broadly being asserted through an understanding of what emergence could bring to architecture (emergence insinuating the complexity that is acquired through the evolution of organisms over time, where the sum is more than the parts), the stress on self-organisation in this issue isolates a particular aspect. The content spirals outwards, as outlined by Hensel in his introduction opposite, clarifying first what self-organisation can mean in the natural world and then discussing its application for material sciences and engineering. There is also further investigation of morphogenetic techniques and technologies, as illustrated by the group's own research and the network they have built up among fellow-minded practitioners in aligning disciplines. While the group's approach is becoming more established and they are boring down effectively into it, their influence is also widening. All three proponents are regularly invited to teach in venerable institutions abroad, with Menges having recently been awarded a professorship of form generation and materialisation in Germany. In 2004, the focus of the group's activities was largely concentrated in the recent establishment of the Masters programme at the aa, but two years later its first few years of graduates are working and spreading the word as practitioners in key firms and other international institutions are buying into this approach and recognising its inherent potential. *D*

Helen Castle

Towards Self-Organisational and Multiple-Performance Capacity in Architecture

Techniques and Technologies in Morphogenetic Design expands and develops the themes of the previous, highly successful *Emergence: Morphogenetic Design Strategies* issue of ⊿ (Vol 74, No 3, 2004), which was also guest-edited by Michael Hensel, Achim Menges and Michael Weinstock of the Emergence and Design Group. While the first volume elucidated the concepts of emergence and self-organisation in relation to the discipline of architecture, this issue augments its theoretical and methodological foundation within a biological paradigm for architectural design, while also discussing promising, related, instrumental techniques for design, manufacturing and construction. **Michael Hensel** introduces the issue and explains how it addresses a much broader range of scales, from the molecular to that of macro-structure and, beyond, to ecological relations.

Coloured X-ray of hyacinth flowers at different stages of growth.
Environmentally sensitive growth can deliver a paradigm for architectural
design, as discussed in 'Computing Self-Organisation' (see page 12).

Robotic timber-manufacturing employed for the 2005 Serpentine Pavilion, as discussed in 'Manufacturing Diversity' (see page 70).

Complex adaptive systems entail processes of self-organisation and emergence. However, both concepts express very different characteristics of a system's behaviour.[1] Self-organisation can be described as a dynamic and adaptive process through which systems achieve and maintain structure without external control. The latter does not preclude extrinsic forces, since all phsycial systems exist within the context of physics, for as long as these do not assert control over intrinsic processes from outside. Common form-finding methods, for example, deploy the self-organisation of material systems exposed to physics to achieve optimisation of performance capacity. Self-organisational systems often display emergent properties or behaviours that arise out of the coherent interaction between lower-level entities, and the aim is to utilise and instrumentalise behaviour as a response to stimuli towards performance-oriented designs.

Both issues of *D* guest-edited by the Emergence and Design Group seek to outline processes of self-organisation and emergence, and to integrate them within a theoretical, methodological and practice-oriented agenda for architectural design. This issue investigates how self-organisation promotes functions and properties of systems through an increase of order, how behaviour and performance capacity arises from these processes, how materials and material systems can be conditioned accordingly, which manufacturing and assembly approaches can facilitate this, and how these processes and approaches can be harnessed for architectural design to achieve a higher level of performativity and, thus, ultimately a higher level of sustainability.

Self-Organisation
The first section focuses on the introduction and discussion of processes of self-organisation based on a biological paradigm, and examines their uses in architectural design.

How do plants grow in relation to multiple extrinsic influences? How can environmentally sensitive growth be instrumentalised in architectural design? What are the available methods and tools, and how can they serve architectural design? Such questions are pursued by Michael Hensel in 'Computing Self-Organisation: Environmentally Sensitive Growth Modelling'. The article examines the work of Professor Prusinkiewicz's team at the Department of Computer Science at the University of Calgary in Alberta, Canada, and explicates its potential value for architectural design.

In '(Synthetic) Life Architectures: Ramifications and Potentials of a Literal Biological Paradigm for Architectural Design', the currently prevailing biological paradigm is taken to its most literal extreme in an inquiry into the consequences of understanding architectures as living entities and the potential benefits of applying life criteria to architecture. Here, Hensel examines recent advances in

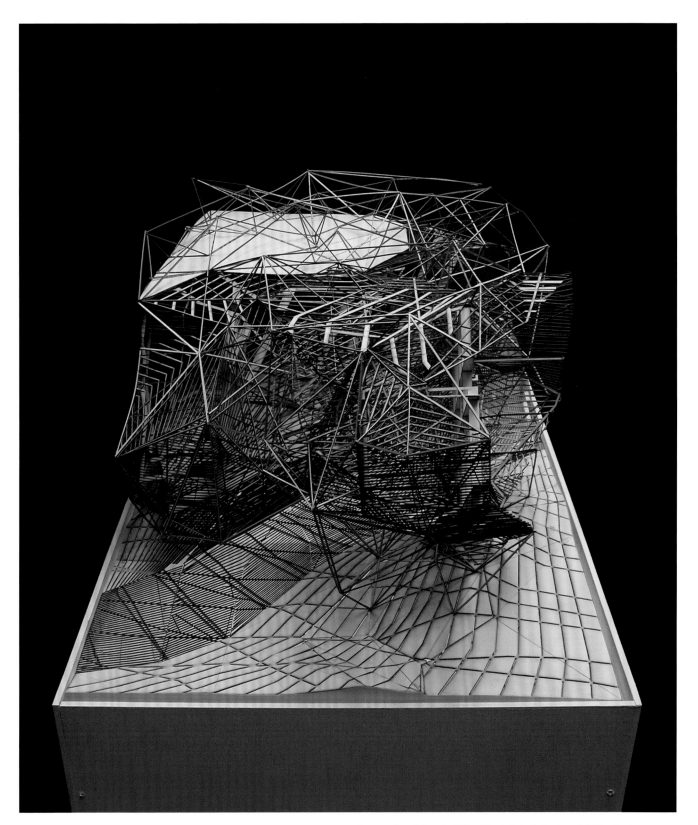

Laser-cut model scale 1/75 of the Jyväskylä Music and Art Centre by OCEAN NORTH, as discussed in 'Differentiation and Performance' (see page 60).

Polymorphism is the state of being made of many different elements, forms, kinds or individuals. In biology it refers to the occurrence of different forms, stages or types in individual organisms or in organisms of the same species. Typogenesis refers to the occurrence of a new type.

Proliferation and differentiation of a digital
parametric component, as discussed in
'Polymorphism ' (see page 78).

Double curvature resulting from differential surface actuation, as discussed in 'Polymorphism' (see page 78).

synthetic life research and their potential implications for, and applications within, architecture.

The engineering principles of biological systems, the high degree of redundancy and complexity in the material hierarchies of many natural structures, and the means by which biological systems respond and adapt to environmental stresses and dynamic loadings, is discussed by Michael Weinstock in 'Self-Organisation and the Structural Dynamics of Plants'. Analysis and case studies reveal that the robust design of natural living systems is not produced by optimisation and standardisation, but by redundancy and differentiation. In this article, Weinstock gives an account of the experimental use of engineering analysis (finite element analysis/FEA) on two plant systems, presents an explanation of the nonlinear dynamics of

natural structures, and suggests the abstraction of these principles for application in architectural engineering.

Recent advances in material science and related innovative methods of producing synthetic materials have had a radical impact on advanced industries, and new composite materials are being 'grown' that have increasingly complex internal structures based on biological models. In 'Self-Organisation and Material Constructions', Weinstock examines the manufacturing of advanced cellular materials informed by concepts of self-organisational processes in biological structures. New cellular materials, such as foamed metals, ceramics, polymers and glass, are indications of a significant change in the design of materials, where the boundaries between the 'natural' and the 'manufactured' begin to be eradicated.

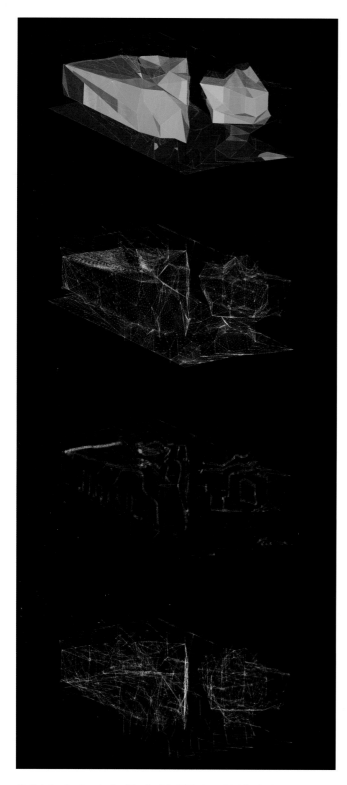

Digital structural analysis of the Jyväskylä Music and Art Centre by OCEAN NORTH, as discussed in 'Differentiation and Performance' (see page 60). From top: Vertical displacement contours for deformation produced by gravity loading; vertical displacement vector plots for deformation produced by gravity loading; plot showing the deformed shape of the structure produced by gravity loading. (Red indicates highest deformation, blue indicates lowest deformation.)

Behaviour

Self-organising systems display capacity for adaptation in the presence of change, an ability to respond to stimuli from the dynamic environment. Irritability facilitates systems with the capacity to adapt to changing circumstances.

Adapting geometry to changing circumstances throughout the design process can be a time-consuming and costly ordeal or, on the other hand, can be anticipated and tools designed that facilitate the possibility of significant changes right up to the manufacturing stage. Whenever the design requirements and constraints and performance profiles of a design change, it is important that the design can absorb such changes through a modifiable geometric modelling setup capable of retaining geometric relations while being substantially modified.

Over the last two decades, the members of the SmartGeometry Group have worked on the conception of such tools, and pioneering new techniques and technologies in the field of computer-aided design (CAD). They are now in key positions in international companies and involved in the development of a new generation of parametric design software. In 'Instrumental Geometry', Achim Menges discusses with SmartGeometry Group members Robert Aish (Director of Research at Bentley Systems), Lars Hesselgren (Director of Research and Development, KPF London), J Parrish (Director of ArupSport) and Hugh Whitehead (Project Director of the Specialist Modelling Group, Foster and Partners, London) the group's instrumental approach to geometry and their unique collaboration based on the careful integration of architectural practice and interrelated software development.

In technology, simulation is the mathematical representation of the interaction of real-world objects. It is essential for designing complex material systems with respect to analysing their behaviour over time. In 'Advanced Simulation in Design', Michael Weinstock and Nikolaos Stathopoulos present a survey of concepts and techniques of advanced simulations within physics and engineering. Simulation is examined as a method for analysing behaviour, including the advanced physics of nonlinear behaviour, and the dynamic changes structures and materials undergo in response to changing conditions. In aerospace and maritime design, as well as automotive engineering, physical behaviour – including wear and fatigue throughout the life of a vehicle – is simulated during the design phase. In numerous industries, manufacturing processes are also simulated digitally during the design phase to facilitate 'virtual' manufacturing, prototyping and construction processes. In this article, a series of examples is used to demonstrate the incorporation of simulation methods and techniques within architectural design.

In biology, differentiation entails the process by which cells or tissues undergo a change towards a more specialised form or function, to become increasingly oriented towards fulfilling specific tasks, to acquire specific performance capacity. In 'Differentiation and Performance: Multiple-Performance Architectures and Modulated Environments', Hensel and Menges argue for an ecological model for architecture that promotes an active modulation of environmental conditions across ranges and over time through morphological differentiation. This approach promises both a new spatial paradigm for architectural design and advanced sustainability that links the performance capacity of material systems with environmental modulation and the resulting provisions and opportunities for inhabitation. Projects by OCEAN NORTH, Neri Oxman and Daniel Coll I Capdevila illustrate different approaches to designing differentiated and multi-performance architectures.

Material Conditioning
Conditioning refers to a learning process in which an organism's behaviour becomes dependent on the occurrence of a stimulus in its environment. In turn, this implies a careful calibration between behavioural and, by extension, performative scope in relation to specific ranges of environmental conditions. The capacity for this can be embedded in the makeup of materials and in the logic of material assemblies. Self-organisational and behavioural capacity of the built environment can thus be facilitated by a related material, manufacturing and assembly approach. This must be based on a related understanding and utilising material characteristics, behaviours and capacities, and ranges from using existing materials in different ways, to using computer-aided manufacturing (CAM) technologies strategically and, finally, to designing materials with greater performance capacities.

Recent developments in digital fabrication and CAM in the building sector have a profound impact on architecture as a material practice by facilitating a much greater and much more differentiated formal and material repertoire for design. In 'Manufacturing Diversity', Achim Menges describes advanced digital manufacturing techniques and technologies for steel, timber and membrane fabrication and construction, and introduces the pioneering work of selected manufacturing companies, including Covertex, Finnforest Merk, Octatube Space Structures, Seele and Skyspan.

Polymorphism is the state of being made of many different elements, forms, kinds or individuals. In biology it refers to the occurrence of different forms, stages or types in individual organisms or in organisms of the same species. Typogenesis refers to the occurrence of a new type. In 'Polymorphism', Menges instrumentalises the two concepts and presents morphogenetic design techniques and technologies that synthesise processes of formation and materialisation. Along a series of designs and design

experiments, undertaken by himself along with Andrew Kudless, David Newton and Joseph Kellner et al, Menges explains an understanding of form, materials and structure as complex interrelations in polymorphic systems that result from the response to extrinsic influences and are materialised by deploying the logics of advanced manufacturing processes as strategic constraints upon the design processes.

In 'Material and Digital Design Synthesis', Michael Hensel and Achim Menges discuss the ramifications of integrating material self-organisation, digital morphogenesis, associative parametric modelling and computer-aided manufacturing into a seamless design process. They describe how the advanced material and morphogenetic digital design techniques and technologies presented call for a higher-level methodological integration, which poses a major challenge for the next generation of multidisciplinary architectural research and projects. This collaborative task encompasses the striving for an integrated set of design methods, generative and analytical tools and enabling technologies that facilitate and instrumentalise evolutionary design and evaluation of differentiated material systems towards a highly performative and sustainable built environment. The article includes works produced within the context of the Emergent Technologies and Design Masters programme at the Architectural Association (AA) in London, and a recent competition entry by Scheffler + Partner Architects and Achim Menges.

Throughout the issue, the authors have listed further references and recommended literature to provide further avenues of enquiry for interested readers. Unfortunately, due to space constraints, many relevant and important references have been omitted. However, since this publication introduces only the beginning of a new approach to multiple-performance-driven and sustainable architectural design, it is hoped that the key spectrum of concepts, methods, techniques and technologies has been presented, and that readers have been inspired to join in the quest to innovate and continue to develop such a morphogenetic design approach. Frei Otto stated that 'it is only of importance that we recognise our future tasks'.[2] It is in this spirit, and with great enthusiasm, that we hope to meet you as collaborators to work together on solving the complex tasks that today's and tomorrow's human environment and state of our biosphere present. ∆

Notes
1. For further elaboration see Tom De Wolf and Tom Holvoet, 'Emergence and Self-Organisation: A Statement of Similarities and Differences', in S Brueckner, G Di Marzo Serugendo, A Karageorgos and R Nagpal (eds), *Proceedings of the International Workshop on Engineering Self-Organising Applications 2004*. www.cs.kuleuven.be/~tomdw/.
2. Frei Otto in conversation with the Emergence and Design Group.

Computing Self-Organisation: Environmentally Sensitive Growth Modelling

The self-organisation processes underlying the growth of living organisms can provide important lessons for architects. Natural systems display higher-level integration and functionality evolving from a dynamic feedback relation with a specific host environment. Biologists, biomimetic engineers and computer scientists have begun to tackle research in this field and there is much to learn from their work. Here, **Michael Hensel** examines the work undertaken by Professor Przemyslaw Prusinkiewicz and his collaborators at the Department of Computer Science at the University of Calgary in Alberta, Canada,[1] outlining its potential application for architectural design.

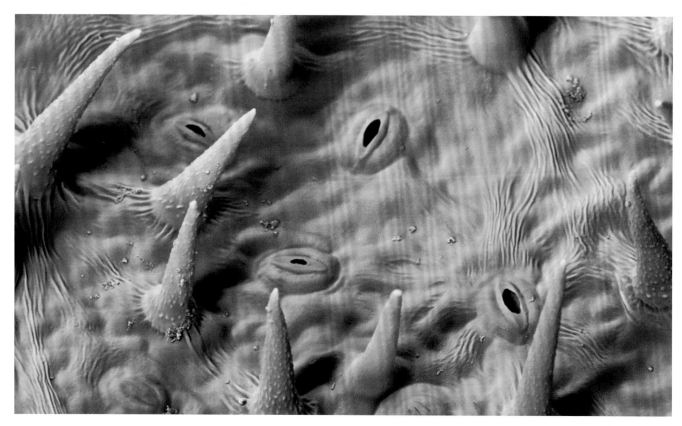

Coloured scanning electron micrograph of the underside of a leaf of the herb lemon balm (*Melissa officinalis*). Numerous hairs, so-called trichomes, cover the undersurface of the leaf. These hairs may have both a protective function against predators and serve to reduce evaporation from the leaf. Stomata, or pores, appear as small, green rounded structures and exchange gases and water from the leaf surface. Magnification: x 900 at 6 x 7 centimetres.

Over the last few decades, visualisation of our environment has profoundly shaped our understanding of it and has yielded entirely new sensibilities. Photos of the earth from outer space enhanced the awareness of climatic and tectonic dynamics and a feel for the planet's fragile balance of flows. Microphotography revealed the most exquisite details of even the smallest organisms and the fine calibration of their size-dependent performance capacities in relation to a specific environmental context. Now there are new visualisation and simulation techniques that focus on self-organisational processes such as environmentally sensitive plant growth. What can be learned from these new methods is not only new sensibilities relative to the visualised processes, but also the specific configurations and features of the tools and their potential contribution in rethinking approaches to design that aim for instrumentalising self-organisation.

Self-organisation is a process in which the internal organisation of a system adapts to the environment to promote a specific function without being guided or managed from outside. In biology this includes the processes that concern developmental biology, which is the study of growth and development of organisms and comprises the genetic control of cell growth, differentiation and morphogenesis. Cell growth encompasses increases both in cell numbers and in cell size. Cellular differentiation describes the process by which cells acquire a 'type'. The morphology of a cell may change dramatically during differentiation. Morphogenesis involves the shapes of tissues, organs and entire organisms and the position of specialised cell types.

When attempting to set forth a paradigm for differentiated and multi-performance architectures, it is interesting to examine available methods for modelling biological growth informed by a hosting environment. Through this investigation it is possible to derive architectural strategies and methods that are informed by environmentally specific conditions and, thus, to achieve advanced levels of functionality and performativity.

Biologists and computational scientists have collaborated on this task with very interesting results. It is possible to evolve plants digitally that are 'grown' according to environmental input. Every change in the input yields a different growth result. In other words, a different articulation of the modelled species. This is called modelling environmentally sensitive growth and could be of interest for architects, in that it could deliver a method and toolset in which design preferences are embedded within a parametric setup, and that is simultaneously informed by a specific environmental and material context. Overall, such an approach would promise an advanced take on sustainability.

The following section introduces the research that has been undertaken in the field of computational modelling of plant growth and development, specifically by Professor Przemyslaw Prusinkiewicz's team at the Department of Computer Science at the University of Calgary, and through their collaborations with other leading experts and institutions, and outlines some of the opportunities for applications in the field of architectural design.

In 1968, the Hungarian biologist Aristid Lindenmayer researched the growth patterns of different, simple multicellular organisms. The same year he began to develop a formal description of the development of such simple organisms, called the Lindenmayer system or L-system.[2] An L-system is what in computer science is called a formal grammar, an abstract structure that describes a formal language through sequences of various simple objects known as strings. For L-system-based plant modelling, these might describe specific modules. There are two categories of formal grammars: analytical and generative. An analytical grammar determines whether a string is a member of the language described by the grammar. A generative grammar formalises

Modelling plant growth and development is predominantly based on mathematical, spatial models that treat plant geometry as a continuum or as discrete components in space. Components might include the local scale of individual plant cells, the regional system scale of modules such as nodes, buds, apices, leaves and so on, or the plant taken as a whole for ecological models.

an algorithm that generates strings in the defined language and consists of a set of rewriting rules for transforming strings, beginning from a single start symbol and applying iteratively the rules to rewrite the string. The specific feature of L-system grammars that allows them to faithfully capture the dynamics of plant growth is that the rewriting rules are applied in parallel to all the symbols in the string at each iteration. For L-system-based plant modelling, the rewriting rules capture, for example, the behaviour of individual modules over predetermined time intervals. The respective language consists of all the strings that can be generated by the given set of rules. This recursive process, which defines L-systems, facilitates the modelling of growth processes of organismal development, such as plant modelling.

Modelling plant growth and development is predominantly based on mathematical, spatial models that treat plant geometry as a continuum or as discrete components in space. Components might include the local scale of individual plant cells, the regional system scale of modules such as nodes, buds, apices, leaves and so on, or the plant taken as a whole for ecological models. Developmental models that describe form as a result of growth are very interesting, as growth-influencing variables can be altered and the resulting changes compared with previous stages. Such models can involve a large number of parameters in calibrated descriptive models of specific plants. Simulations produce numerical output, which can be complemented by rendered images and animations for the purpose of easily comprehensible visualisation.

According to Professor Prusinkiewicz, the use of computational models has several benefits. Firstly, they can

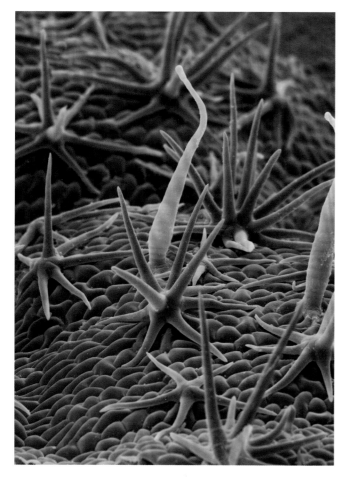

Coloured scanning electron micrograph of the differentiated leaf surface and leaf hairs of the rock (or sun) rose (*Cistus longifolius*). These trichomes guard the leaf against attack by pests, the glandular hairs, shown in yellow, producing defensive chemicals, while the other hairs shown in grey provide mechanical protection. Magnification: x 125 at 6 x 6 centimetres.

'provide quantitative understanding of developmental mechanisms; secondly, models might lead to a synthetic understanding of the interplay between various aspects of development'.[3] In doing so, such models might also provide a new analytical and generative sensibility to architectural design, as they may facilitate a much better understanding of synergies between systems and environments, or subsystem interaction, in terms of their behavioural characteristics and capacities with respect to the purpose they serve locally and within the behavioural economy of a larger system.

Professor Prusinkiewicz speaks of 'models of plant architecture based on the ecological concept of a plant as a population of semi-autonomous modules … describing a growing plant as an integration of the activities of these modules'. He identifies the specifically useful feature of L-systems as the capacity to 'give rise to a class of programming languages for specifying the models [which] makes it possible to construct generic simulation software that is capable of modelling a large variety of plants at the architectural level, given their specifications in an L-system-based language. Entire model specifications, as well as model parameters, can easily be manipulated in simulation experiments.'[4] Such architectural models can be used for the modelling of entire plants, or groups of plants, potentially embedded within a given ecology, or of various parts and subscales of a single plant.

With respect to the modelling of individual plants, one of the most striking features is the integration of biomechanics into plant development, which allows informing the plant growth with extrinsic physical, biological and environmental input. Advanced models incorporate the combined impact of gravity, tropism, contact between the various elements of a plant structure and contact with obstacles.[5] The methodological setup, the toolset and the choice of determining variables are equally interesting for architectural design. Entire building systems and envelopes could thus be informed by multivariable input and optimised to satisfy multi-performance objectives. The gravity input can inform structural behaviour that is then negotiated with exposure to environmental input, for example to collect sun energy, rainwater and so on. Instead of a step-by-step, objective-by-objective optimisation at the end of the design process, undertaken by specialists who are not central to the design process, response to extrinsic stimuli can now be a part of the generative process of architecture. What might require some work is the way in which physics are integrated in the toolset beyond the purpose of visualisation, and how the output of each stage might tie into necessary analytical methods and processes.

The software developed by the Calgary team enables various plant characteristics to be modelled. These include spiral phyllotaxis, which serves to optimise the packing of seeds or scales, or the orientation and exposure of leaves towards environmental input such as sunlight.[6] This is of particular interest for architecture as it enables an informed distribution of specific performative architectural features – for example, energy-generating photovoltaic or photosynthetic elements – over a building envelope that is at the same time optimised towards multiple objectives, including the way the elements populate the building envelope relative to its overall orientation to multiple input sources, such as sun path, prevailing wind directions, and so on. Plants are capable of doing precisely this. Hair on plants, often organised in phyllotactic distribution like thorns or other such features, fulfils various functions, such as repelling water from plant stems that would otherwise rot, or repelling feeding animals through toxins contained within the hair. A very interesting function is that provided by hair around the stomata of leaves. In this case, hair modulates airflow so that leaves and plants do not lose too much water through the combination of evaporation and transpiration. This often occurs in locations that experience severe weather conditions, such as coastal climates affected by gale-force winds.

It is remarkable how such tiny features on plants manage to modulate very strong forces in such a way that the plant can survive rather extreme conditions. The lesson here for architects is that these features and their functions do not scale. However, there are two ways in which one can utilise the lesson learned from living nature: first by producing same-size features to achieve the performance observed in nature, and second to determine appropriate sizes for other features to modulate chosen conditions over required ranges. With respect to the methodological approach, very small features such as hair on plants can be mapped onto plant models. The Calgary team achieves this by generating plant skeletons using L-systems and then graphically interpreting these as generalised cylinders. Hair properties are then specified and the hair mapped onto the surface and adjusted according to positional information.[7] Interestingly, standard software such as 3D studio and Cinema 4D have recently incorporated hair simulation in relation to airflow, in such a way that specific properties of hair and airflow can be determined. While this was initially important for the film industry – for example, to produce effective hair simulation for films like *King Kong* – these tools can now be of great value in architectural design. Analysis and design generation can thus again be synthesised.

Modelling growth processes that are sensitive to system-extrinsic influences and negotiated with system-intrinsic organisational information and related features hold great potential for architecture with respect to evolving buildings from similar processes. This suggests an expansion of the endeavour to incorporate ecological organisation and relations. Ecology is the study of the relation of organism to their hosting environment, which can be studied at various levels ranging from the individual organism to populations, communities of species, ecosystems and, finally, the biosphere.

At the level of the individual organism or species, there is the study of behavioural ecology. Behaviour is an observable action or response of an organism or species to environmental factors. Behavioural ecology entails, therefore, the ecological and evolutionary basis for behaviour and the roles of behaviour in enabling organisms to adapt to their ecological niches. It concerns individual organisms and how these organisms are affected by (and how they can affect) their biotic and abiotic environment. This involves: firstly, a stimulus, in other words an internal or external agent that

Phyllotaxis (Greek *phyllo*: leaf + *taxis*: arrangement) is the study of the arrangement of repeated plant units and the pattern of their repetition within the same alignment. These include leaves arranged around a stem, scales on a cone or pineapple, florets in the head of a daisy, and seeds in a sunflower.
Spiral phyllotaxis is a phyllotactic pattern where the elements are arranged as a spiral lattice, an arrangement of points on concentric circles with a radius increasing at a constant rate and with a constant (divergence) angle between successive points. The photo shows a Menzies Banksia (*Banksia Menziesii*) seed cone. Menzies Banksia is a shrub that produces large red flower spikes. After pollination, the seeds are produced in this cone-like structure. The cone shows a finely detailed spiral phyllotactic pattern of its unit arrangement, modified, yet not disrupted, by the larger features of the openings for seed release.

produces a reaction or change in an organism; secondly, sensibility, which is the capacity to perceive a stimulus; and thirdly, sensitivity which is the capacity of an organism to respond to stimuli. The last is regarded as a property common to all life forms and is also called 'irritability'. The related processes of sensing, growth and actuation are often embedded capacities within the material make-up of living nature. The modelling of context-sensitive growth processes described above is based on this understanding and incorporates it in its methodological setup.

The next level concerns populations or, in other words, all organisms that constitute a specific group and occur in a specific habitat. Population ecology involves the dynamic of populations within species, and the interaction of these populations with environmental factors. The level concerning communities, which are species that interact with one another in a specific region under relatively similar environmental conditions, is called community ecology, and encompasses the interaction between species within an ecological community and their shared environment.

For population- and community-level ecologies, the Calgary team developed interesting simulation tools that generate spatial distributions for plant communities. There is a considerable level of complexity involved in the modelling of ecosystems, including the geometric articulation of individuals and their particular features, which needs to be consistent with their position within the ecosystem and the related environmental input, as well as the interaction between species and with a specific environment. For this purpose, the team combined two types of models into a bidirectional one that incorporates, first, a local-to-global direction comprising an ecosystem simulation based on individual plants and their proliferation and distribution and, second, a global-to-local direction, which infers positions of individual plants from a given distribution of plant densities. This is then further informed by a specific pattern of clustering and succession of plants. However, rather than the integration of all data into one single and very complex detailed model, a multilevel approach was developed. A higher-level model determines the distribution of plants, while a lower-level model determines the plants' shapes and features.[8]

While this type of modelling might have obvious theoretical and practical applications for biologists, it holds similar potential for architects and urban designers. One application might involve the distribution of buildings specific to a given environment. Depending on their particular interaction with the environment, buildings can be distributed and clustered in appropriate ways, so as to accumulate or disperse the effects of their interaction and its impact on the evolution of their further relationship. A further application might concern the distribution of building elements or features across a larger building envelope. This

Model of rose campion (*Lychnis coronaria*) expressed using a context-free L-system generated with L-Studio, a software package developed at the Department of Computer Science at the University of Calgary.

ties in an obvious way into the modelling described above.

While these two approaches operate on a discreet and divided relationship between buildings, and buildings and their environment, or interior and exterior space, a third approach introduces a different proliferation mode that challenges and disentangles this artificial dichotomy. As many plants grow wherever conditions are beneficial, irrespective of seams that divide entities or surfaces they grow on, so could elements of the built environment be distributed according to performance-based criteria, instead of adhering to the potentially disadvantageous constraint of ownership or exterior/interior thresholds. A fairly trivial example would be a distribution of photovoltaic elements that is informed by required performance-based orientation and density into a local mat or patchwork irrespective of ownership boundaries. With systems overlapping ownership boundaries, several questions arise as to who owns what, who pays for what and who is liable for what. Some answers to these questions already exist with respect to the status and supply of current building infrastructure and energy, and one could easily start building on the existing rules and regulations. By and large, this approach delivers a very different understanding of entities and conditions of the built environment, away from the discreetness of elements towards the synergetic interrelation between environmentally sensitive and performance-oriented growth processes and their time- and context-specific output.

Our human biosphere could only benefit from an approach towards multi-performance systems distributed according to a related logic and facilitated by rigorous performance-oriented modelling tools. ⌀

Thanks to Martin Hemberg for expert advice.

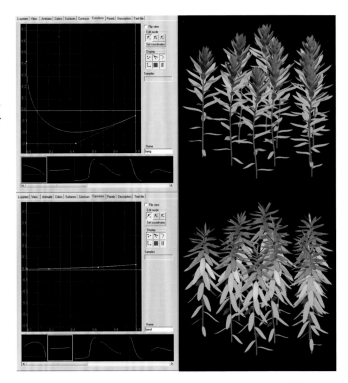

Model of Indian paintbrush field generated with L-Studio. L-studio is Windows software for creating simulation models and performing virtual experiments using L-systems. The software consists of L-system-based simulators, editors and other modelling tools for creating and modifying objects, and environmental programs that simulate environmental processes that affect plant development.

Notes
1. Information on Professor Przemyslaw Prusinkiewicz's team at the Department of Computer Science at the University of Calgary, including articles and software downloads (Virtual Laboratory for Unix or L-Studio for Windows) can be found at: http://algorithmicbotany.org.
2. See Aristid Lindenmayer, 'Mathematical models for cellular interaction in development', *Journal of Theoretical Biology* 18, 1968.
3. See Przemyslaw Prusinkiewicz, 'Modelling plant growth and development', in Vivian Irish and Philip Benfey (eds), *Current Opinions in Plant Biology 2004*, Special Issue: *Growth and Development*, Elsevier, 2004.
4. ibid.
5. See Catherine Jirasek, Przemyslaw Prusinkiewicz and Bruno Moulina,

'Integrating biomechanics into developmental plant models expressed using L-systems', in H Ch Spatz and T Speck (eds), *Plant Biomechanics 2000, Proceedings of the 3rd Plant Biomechanics Conference 2000*, Georg Thieme Verlag (Stuttgart), 2000.
6. See Deborah Fowler, Przemyslaw Prusinkiewicz and Johannes Battjes, 'A collision-based model of spiral phyllotaxis', from the proceedings of SIGGRAPH '92, in *Computer Graphics*, 26 (2), July 1992.
7. See Martin Fuhrer, Henrik Jensen and Przemyslaw Prusinkiewicz, 'Modelling hairy plants', *Proceedings of Pacific Graphics*, 2004.
8. See Brendan Lane and Przemyslaw Prusinkiewicz, 'Generating spatial distributions for multi-level models of plant communities', *Proceedings of Graphics Interface*, Calgary, 2002.

Further Reading
Aristid Lindenmayer, 'Mathematical models for cellular interaction in development', *Journal of Theoretical Biology* 18, 1968.
Aristid Lindenmayer and Przemyslaw Prusinkiewicz, *The Algorithmic Beauty of Plants*, Springer Verlag (London, New York), 1990.
Oliver Deussen, Pat Hanrahan, Bernd Lintermann, Mech Radomir, Matt Pharr and Przemyslaw Prusinkiewicz, 'Realistic modelling and rendering of plant ecosystems', from the proceedings of SIGGRAPH '98, Orlando, Florida, 1998.
Una-May O'Reilly, Martin Hemberg and Achim Menges, 'Evolutionary computation and artificial life in architecture: Exploring the potentials of generative and genetic algorithms as operative design tools', ⌀ Emergence: Morphogenetic Design Strategies, Vol 74, No 3, 2004, pp 48–53.

(Synthetic) Life Architectures: Ramifications and Potentials of a Literal Biological Paradigm for Architectural Design

Biology is the science of life. It concerns itself with the living. The long-proclaimed biological paradigm for architectural design must for this reason go beyond using shallow biological metaphors or a superficial biomorphic formal repertoire. The consequence is a literal understanding of the design product as a synthetic life-form embedded within dynamic and generative ecological relations. **Michael Hensel** examines the repercussions of this proposition and surveys current developments in biology and biochemistry with respect to synthetic-life research, gathering insights into their potential application in architectural design.

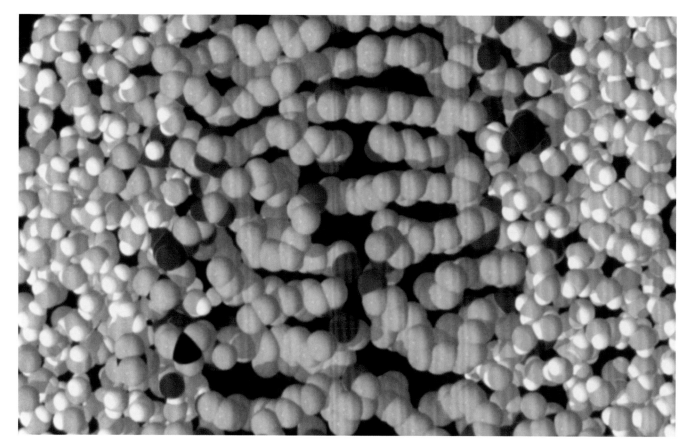

Molecular graphic of the phospholipid bilayer that forms the membrane around all living cells. The cell membrane is made of phospholipid molecules, each of which has a hydrophilic (soluble in water) and hydrophobic (insoluble in water) end. The hydrophobic part of the phospholipid is a fatty-acid chain, shown here in blue. The molecules line up in two sheets, with the fatty-acid chains forming a hydrophobic layer in the middle. The hydrophilic surface on both sides of the membrane, shown here in yellow and white, is the point of contact for molecules leaving or entering the cell.

To pursue seriously the proposition of synthetic-life architectures it is important to take a close look at biological processes and materials, all the way down to the molecular scale, involving biochemistry in the understanding of the advanced functionality and performance capacity of biological organisms. The composite material organisation of biological structures is typically morphologically and functionally defined across a minimum of eight scales of magnitude, ranging from the nano- to the macro-scale. While inherent functionality is scale dependent, it is nevertheless interrelated and interdependent across scales of magnitude. It is, in effect, nonlinear: the whole is more than the sum of the parts. A central role is played by processes of self-organisation and the functional properties that emerge from them.

Self-organisation is a process in which the internal organisation of a system increases automatically without being guided or managed by an external source. It is central to the description of biological systems, from subcellular to ecosystems. Self-organising systems typically display emergent properties, which arise when a number of simple entities or agents cooperate in an environment, forming more complex behaviours as a collective. Emergent properties arise when a complex system reaches a combined threshold of diversity, organisation and connectivity.

Thanks to biomimetic engineering, the strategic consideration of the interrelated make-up and functionality of biological materials is slowly beginning to make its way into architectural design. However, in relation to architecture, thus far this concerns, at best, the arrangement and properties of fibres and matrix in anisotropic composite materials. It would seem logical and necessary to also include the molecular scale, which promises to yield a functionality of an as yet unrealised extent and to make possible advanced performativity and sustainability. Such an approach would involve biochemistry, the discipline concerned with the study of molecules and their chemistry in reactions that facilitate the processes that make living systems possible.

An inquiry into synthetic-life research reveals a broad range of activities and involved institutions. The Programmable Artificial Cell Evolution (PACE) project, for example, is an integrated project funded by the European Commission and is made up of 14 European and US universities and businesses. Together these organisations pursue research related to the development of artificial cells and methods to programme their chemical functions. The PACE project aims at creating the foundation for an embedded information technology using programmable, self-assembling artificial cells.[1] One of its members, the European Center for Living Technology (ECLT), based in Venice, conducts research and training for scientists and engineers with the aim of utilising programmable artificial-cell evolution, and hosts public debates on the social, ethical and safety issues related to living technology.[2] And ProtoLife,

While some of the PACE research teams attempt to create synthetic life from existing biochemical structures that can be found in biological organisms, others try to create synthetic life from compounds that do not occur in living nature. However, whatever their approach, it must be based on fulfilling criteria on the basis of which it can be established whether something is alive or not.

also based in Venice, is dedicated to the development of 'evolutionary chemistry with the long-range goal of creating artificial cells from nonliving raw material, and programming them with desired chemical functionality'.[3]

Protocell Assembly, a project sponsored by the Los Alamos National Laboratory, 'seeks to assemble a minimal self-replicating molecular machine', and focuses on the conditions under which simple synthetic life-forms can be assembled. According to its mission statement: 'The project seeks to develop the underpinning science for the assembly of functional proto-cells, ie simple self-reproducing nano-systems that can perform useful tasks.'[4] The Los Alamos team is currently attempting to achieve a synthetic life-form nick-named the 'Los Alamos Bug'.

While some of the PACE research teams attempt to create synthetic life from existing biochemical structures that can be found in biological organisms, others try to create synthetic life from compounds that do not occur in living nature. However, whatever their approach, it must be based on fulfilling criteria on the basis of which it can be established whether something is alive or not.

In 1971, the Hungarian chemical engineer and biologist Tibor Gánti provided a ground-breaking elaboration of life criteria in his seminal work *The Principles of Life*,[5] in which he distinguished between real or absolute life criteria and potential life criteria. According to Gánti, the former are necessary for an organism to be in a living state, while the latter are necessary for the organism's survival in the living world. Real-life criteria are: 1) inherent unity – a system must be inherently an individual unit; 2) metabolism – a living system has to perform metabolism; 3) inherent stability – a living system must be inherently stable; 4) an information-carrying subsystem – a living system must have a subsystem carrying information that is useful for the whole system; 5) programme control – processes in living systems must be

Coloured scanning electron micrograph of a section through the leaf of the Christmas rose (*Helleborus niger*). In the body of the leaf in the centre of the image are numerous cells containing chloroplasts (green). These are small organelles that are the site of photosynthesis within the leaf. Photosynthesis is the process by which plants use sunlight to turn carbon dioxide into sugars. Magnification: x 750 at 4 x 5 inch.

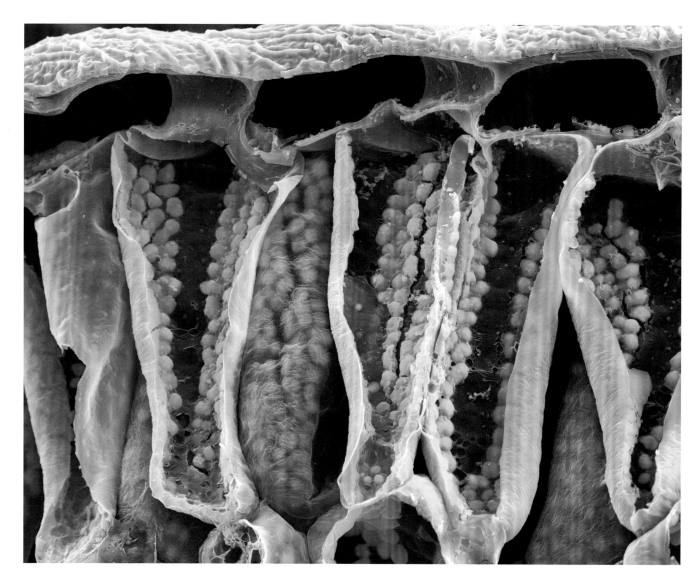

regulated and controlled. Potential life criteria are: 1) growth and reproduction; 2) the capability of hereditary change and evolution; 3) mortality. Synthetic-life research embraces a similar, if abbreviated, list of criteria, including containment (inherent unity), metabolism, heredity and evolution.[6] Synthetic life must fulfil these criteria, driven by deep self-organisational capacity that reaches across the involved scales of magnitude of articulation of biological materials. These criteria are further examined below, and their current or potential application discussed in relation to their prospective use for architecture.

Containment

Containment implies that a system must be inherently an individual unit, a function provided by biological membranes. These are structures composed mostly of lipid and protein that form the external boundary of cells and of major structures within cells. A lipid bilayer membrane is a membrane composed only of lipid. Lipid bilayer is the

foundation of all biological membranes, and is a precondition of cell-based life. A lipid is an organic compound that is insoluble in nonpolar organic solvent. Lipids, together with carbohydrates and proteins, constitute the principal structural materials of living cells. The basic functions of cell membranes are to provide for integrity of the cell: that is, in general, to separate the outside from the inside, as well as carrying out intelligent filtration of material through the membrane. While water and a few other substances, such as carbon and oxygen, can diffuse across the membrane, most molecules necessary for cellular functions traverse the membrane by means of transport mechanisms. Information can also be transmitted across the membrane: specific membrane proteins, so-called receptors, bind hormones or other such informational molecules and subsequently transmit a signal to the interior of the cell.

As membranes form the boundary between cytoplasm and the surrounding environment, they are affected by

Algal bloom turning waves green on the Gulf of Tadjoura, Djibouti, near the Red Sea. The green colour of the water is due to millions of marine algae, microscopic plants that increase in number between spring and autumn due to increased levels of sunlight. Algae are available in great abundance and can be grown and used in artificial photosynthesis technologies to provide the built environment with energy and the means to improve the environment.

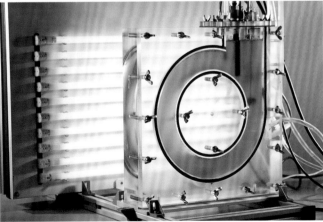

Bioreactor using algae (green) to produce hydrogen gas for use as a fuel. The light source fuels the growth of the algae. Burning hydrogen produces water vapour and is a cleaner source of energy than burning fossil fuels like coal, gas and oil. Photographed in 2003, at the University of Nantes, France.

environmental stresses from the exterior as well as the pathogenic processes from the interior of the cell. The continuous control of chemical processes in membranes typically involves three components: first, a sensor that will provide a response to the chemical whose concentration is to be controlled; second, a controller that translates the response provided by a sensor into a signal that is then transmitted to an actuator; and third, an actuator that will drive the controlling mechanism. Systems combining all three components exist in living cells. Ligan-gated ion channels, for example, are protein molecules that are embedded in the plasma membrane of the cells, and respond to the presence of a biological molecule by opening a channel in the cell membrane that allows a selective passage of ions through the hydrophobic membrane.

Scientists at a number of universities are currently conducting research into membrane materials that incorporate biological molecules capable of selective

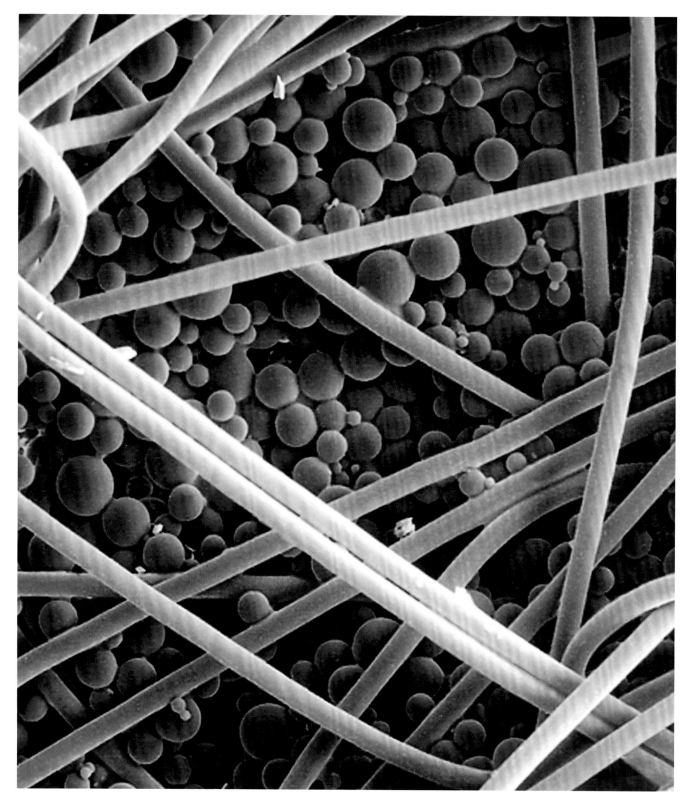

Coloured scanning electron micrograph of microcapsules (blue) that contain a phase-change material (PCM) coating fabric fibres. The PCM can absorb and release heat generated by a person wearing the fabric, warming or cooling it as required. If the wearer's body temperature rises after exercise, the PCM absorbs the heat and melts, preventing heat reflecting back onto the body. If the wearer's temperature then falls, the PCM refreezes, releasing its absorbed heat and warming the garment. The PCM can undergo this melting/refreezing cycle almost indefinitely. PCMs are being developed by Outlast Technologies, US. Magnification unknown.

recognition of a specific signal in such a manner that the membrane will respond by changing its porosity. This change enables other molecules to permeate the membrane. In so doing, the flux through the membrane will be controlled at a local level without the need for central control. While biomembranes are currently not available on a scale relevant to the building industry, the current research is nevertheless promising and includes smart biological membranes that can interact with their environment based on self-assembling biological structures and polymers.[7] Current scales of applications encompass mainly micro-filtration and gaseous diffusion. Medical research focuses on coating for therapeutic agents that can release drugs in response to the condition of the patients, or self-repairing coating in replacement joints.

With research progressing at such a fast pace, biological membranes could deliver a completely new level of interaction and exchange between exterior and interior environments through programmable intelligent filtration and distribution on a molecular scale. In combination with metabolic processes, this might entail the removal of pollutants and improvement of the quality of air and water in both the exterior and interior environments.

Metabolism

Metabolism encompasses the physical and biochemical processes that occur within a living organism that are necessary for the maintenance of life. The biological purpose of metabolism is the production and storing of usable energy. Metabolism entails that organic molecules necessary for life are synthesised from simpler precursors in a process called anabolism, while other complex substances are broken down into simpler molecules in a process called catabolism, so as to yield energy for vital processes. Photosynthesis is the qualitatively and quantitatively most important biochemical process on the planet. The entire energy-dependent process called 'life' is enabled through photosynthesis. The process entails the conversion of energy in sunlight to chemical forms of energy that can be used in biological systems. More specifically it is a biochemical process in which plants, algae and some bacteria harness energy from light to produce food. Carbohydrates are synthesised from carbon dioxide and water using light as an energy source. Most forms of photosynthesis release oxygen as a by-product. Nearly all living beings depend on the oxygen and energy production from photosynthesis for their survival.

The process has been studied in great detail and photosynthetic systems are frequently used for the development and application of advanced technologies. Artificial photosynthesis attempts to replicate the natural process of photosynthesis, converting sunlight and carbon dioxide into carbohydrates and oxygen. One of its potential applications is clean fuel production, such as hydrogen –

the burning of which yields only water and energy – and the conversion of carbon dioxide into organic material and oxygen. On an industrial scale, this possibility might have a dramatic effect upon sustainability and climatic phenomena, for example global warming.

Harnessing artificial photosynthesis might eventually lead to self-sufficient and zero-pollution buildings that are independent from centralised energy-grids and improve their hosting environment. Future applications for artificial photosynthesis are within the solar-energy field (silicone-based technologies require a highly energy-intensive production process and are less efficient in energy output), the production of enzymes and pharmaceuticals, bioremediation, which entails the clean-up of environmental pollutants, and the production of clean-burning fuels such as hydrogen.

Several lines of research currently under way seek to deliver feasible technologies. The main goals are to overcome the energy-consuming production and use of silicon-based photovoltaic cells and the mechanics needed to orient them in an optimal way to the sun path over time. Light photosynthesis-capable membranes are a promising direction for further development. Others include the use of living organisms, such as algae and bacteria.[8] Thus synthetic metabolism has the potential to provide the energy needed for all significant synthetic-life processes. Synthetic-life architectures, fuelled by artificial

Frozen vials containing fragments of DNA known as BioBricks. Each BioBrick performs a specific function and is combined with others to produce novel forms of genetically altered cells. These cells are designed in the same manner as electronic circuits. This new field of genetic engineering is known as synthetic biology and is a simpler method of producing genetically modified cells. In the future, synthetic biology may be used to create new drugs, biosensors and biological computers, or diagnose diseases. Photographed at Massachusetts Institute of Technology, US.

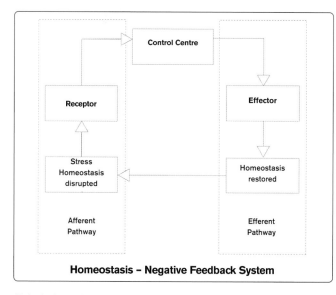

Homeostasis – Negative Feedback System

Biological organisms rely on controlling and stabilising internal conditions through homeostasis, a process controlled by negative feedback. When a state of disruption or stress is registered by receptors, the information is sent to the control centre, which evaluates it and sends a signal to an effector that restores homeostasis.

photosynthesis, might generate their entire energy-requirement from this process, provide a whole series of useful by-products and contribute to cleaning environmental pollutants.

Homeostasis

Homeostasis is a property of open systems, especially living organisms, which regulates their internal environment so as to maintain required stable conditions: for example, stable body temperature. The technical equivalents are thermostats. This commonly involves negative feedback, by which positive and negative control is exerted over the values of a variable or set of variables, and without which control of the system would cease to function. Like the previous criteria, homeostatic systems require sensors to measure the parameters being regulated: signal transmission to a local or global control centre where the deviations from desired values are measured; control centres – if the measured values are different from the set points then signals are sent to effectors to bring the values back to the needed levels; and effectors capable of responding to a stimulus.

The range of biological and available technical sensors, detectors, transducers and actuators is impressively broad.[9] Furthermore, technological setups that can facilitate conditions of homeostasis in a simple negative feedback are often so ubiquitous that one no longer takes notice of them, for as long as they work well. Overall, there are two main questions. First, which stimulus or range of stimuli needs to be registered and transmitted to effectors or actuators to yield a desired response? Second, how to develop technologies that operate more on biochemical principles than mechanical ones, so that the required functionality can be embedded into the material make-up of a synthetic-life architecture? In addition, it might be useful for architectural design to consider negative as well as positive feedback, beyond the criterion of homeostasis, to include responsiveness that can both stabilise or yield change in conditions and behaviours.

Heredity + Evolution

In biology, heredity entails the conveyance of biological characteristics from a parent organism to offspring through genes. Evolution entails change in the genetic composition of a population across successive generations. This is posited as the result of natural selection acting on the genetic variation among individuals, which, over time, results in the development of new species. The research team that is building the Los Alamos Bug posits that if containment, metabolism and genome (heredity) fit together, they should provide the basis for evolution. Evolution is thus seen as an emergent process, the capacity for which may be provided by the correct functional relation and calibration between containment, metabolism and heredity, together with the necessary capability of reproduction.

Growth and reproduction, so argues the Los Alamos team, will yield natural selection, favouring, for example, the individuals that can perform metabolic processes most effectively. This argument suggests that evolution can be understood in some way as a process of optimisation of functionality and performance capacity. Biological systems are, however, so complex that it is often still too difficult to deduce optimisation criteria and constraints in such a way that optimisation goals could be defined. Moreover, biological systems are characterised by multiple-performance capacities across ranges facilitated by the interaction of subsystems across a minimum of eight scales of magnitude. Disentangling this into single-objective optimisation goals is not only difficult, but also simply the wrong approach. Interdependent subsystem functionality results in higher-level integration and functionality. Again, the whole is more than the sum of its parts. Learning this from living nature is already a major achievement for architectural design that will yield new methods of analysis and design generation. However, above and beyond the methodological retooling is the question of how to embed this capacity within, or yield it from, materials and for which purpose.

This brings us back to the criterion of heredity. The challenge is how to embed information within a material so that it can be both passed on and evolve, and to achieve reproduction in order to yield evolution. Particularly interesting here is the Los Alamos team's approach to this problem. Its 'bug' features short strands of peptide nucleic acid (PNA) that carries the genetic information. Like DNA, PNA is

It is precisely the complex and dynamic exchange between an organism and its environment, and the functionality that evolves from it, that makes synthetic life interesting for architecture. Understandably, the very notion of architecture that is alive may sound scary to some and blasphemous to others. However, what is proposed here is not a version of Mary Shelley's *Modern Prometheus*. Instead, it involves embedding into buildings the biochemical processes and functionality of life for the advantage of humans, other species and the environment.

made of two strands. Due to their chemical characteristics and specific 'environmental' conditions, these strands can combine or separate into single strands. Single strands have the ability to attract fragments of matching PNA from their 'environment'. Doubling, splitting and attracting new fragments is a very simple form of reproduction and heredity.

Returning to the question of evolution towards higher levels of performance capacity, it is interesting to consider the field of smart material research. One definition is that 'smart materials and structures are those objects that sense environmental events, process that sensory information, and then act on the environment'.[10] In stable environments this capacity would neither be of use, nor would it depend on evolution to adjust to changing stimuli. Life and its evolution depend on the exchange between organisms and a dynamic environment. To make any sense, smart materials would also need the capacity to evolve, in order not to be immediately redundant if there was an environmental change beyond their capacity to respond in a manner that is in some way beneficial for the overall system. Material research and biochemistry need to cross-inform one another to deliver smart materials that deserve this label. Obviously there is a lot of work to be done in this field before specific industrial applications can be delivered.

In general, there is, of course, the added difficulty of not only fulfilling the above-introduced life criteria, but also of linking them into an interdependent process that amounts to synthetic life. Moreover, the hierarchical functional

organisation of biological organisms across a vast range of scales of magnitude must be seen in relation to a specific context: in other words, to the numerous scalar interrelations within and between ecological systems. Ecology is the branch of biological science that studies the distribution and abundance of living organisms, as well as the interactions between organisms and their environment. Environment is a collective term for the conditions in which an organism lives. It encompasses the complex physical, chemical and biological surroundings that make up the habitat of an organism at any given time.

It is precisely the complex and dynamic exchange between an organism and its environment, and the functionality that evolves from it, that makes synthetic life interesting for architecture. Understandably, the very notion of architecture that is alive may sound scary to some and blasphemous to others. However, what is proposed here is not a version of Mary Shelley's *Modern Prometheus*. Instead, it involves embedding into buildings the biochemical processes and functionality of life for the advantage of humans, other species and the environment. One might think of it as a highly performative synthesis between house and garden embedded within its specific micro-environments and niches and embedded within macro-ecological systems. This promises a powerful, if partial, solution to increasing environmental problems at a time when governments continue to place economic development over environmental concerns, in the face of a world climate that might have begun to go bonkers. ⚙

Notes
1. For PACE see http://134.147.93.66/bmcmyp/Data/PACE/Public.
2. For ECLT see http://bruckner.biomip.rub.de/bmcmyp/Data/ECLT/Public/.
3. For ProtoLife see http://www.protolife.net. See also Bob Holmes, 'Alive! The race to create life from scratch', *New Scientist*, Issue 2486, 12 February 2005.
4. See http://www.protocell.org.
5. Tibor Gánti, *The Principles of Life*, Oxford University Press (Oxford), 2003, first published in Hungarian as *Az élet princípiuma*, Gondolat (Budapest), 1971.
6. Bob Holmes, op cit, pp 28–33.
7. For further information see, for example, the Biochemical and Biomedical Engineering Research Group at Bath University http://www.bath.ac.uk/chemeng/research/groups/babe.shtml.
8. For a detailed elaboration, see Werner Nachtigall, *Bionik: Grundlagen und Beispiele für Ingenieure und Naturwissenschafter*, 2nd edn, Springer Verlag (Berlin, Heidelberg, New York), 2002, pp 318–36.
9. See Michelle Addington and Daniel Schodek, *Smart Materials and Technologies for the Architecture and Design Professions: Elements and Control Systems*, Architectural Press (London, New York), 2005, pp 109–37.
10. John J Kroschwitz (ed), *Encyclopaedia of Chemical Technology*, John Wiley & Sons (London), 1992.

Further Reading:
Tibor Gánti, *The Principles of Life*, Oxford University Press (Oxford), 2003.
Werner Nachtigall, *Bionik: Grundlagen und Beispiele für Ingenieure und Naturwissenschafter*, 2nd edn, Springer Verlag (Berlin, Heidelberg, New York), 2002.
Philip L Yeagle (ed), *The Structure of Biological Membranes*, 2nd edn, CRC Press (London), 2005.

Self-Organisation and the Structural Dynamics of Plants

Classical engineering is driven by efficiency, with a precise economy of materials and structures for specific conditions. **Michael Weinstock** explains how, conversely, biology has evolved redundancy as a deep strategy, with hierarchical arrangements of cells and tissues producing sufficient excess capacity for adaptation to changing environmental stresses. He explains how, with the assistance of George Jeronimidis and Nikolaos Stathopoulos, the Emtech masters programme at the Architectural Association (AA) has explored the integrated morphologies of plants, an analysis that reveals new models for engineered structures.

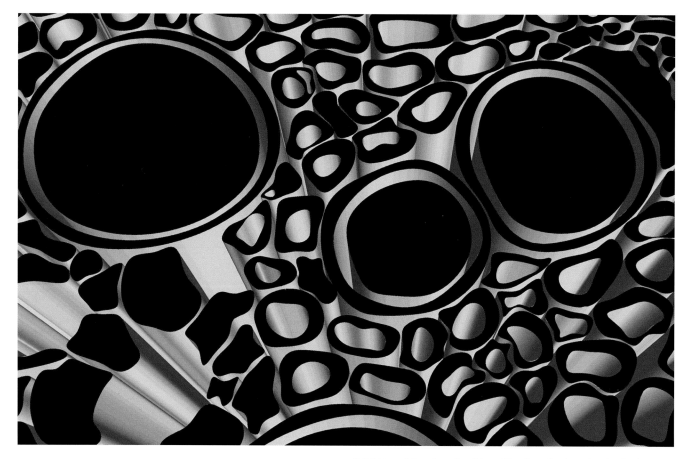

Detailed model section of an internal bamboo structure showing the long cylindrical cells (parenchyma), fibres and xylem (hollow fluid-conducting tubes) that make up the stem. The sectional model is reconstructed from electron-microscope information.

The study of the organisation of materials in biological structures has, until recently, proceeded from the widely accepted view that evolution develops – over very long time periods – optimised, efficient and strong structures. Evolutionary theory has been co-opted to support a view of biological systems that does not contest traditional engineering concepts, particularly the concepts of efficiency and optimisation. This way of thinking is very limited, and ignores both the high degree of redundancy and complexity in the material hierarchies of many natural structures, and the means by which biological systems respond and adapt to environmental stresses and dynamic loadings.[1]

The engineering principles of biological systems can be abstracted and applied to the design of artefacts and buildings, a process known as biomimetics. To do so requires a deeper engagement with evolutionary development and a more systematic analysis of the material organisation[2] and behaviour of individual species. Biological systems are self-assembled, using mainly quite weak materials to make strong structures, and their dynamic responses and properties are very different to the classical engineering of manmade structures. The behaviour of all natural systems is complex and adaptive, and plants in particular manage their structural behaviour in a way that provides new models for engineered structures. Plants resist gravity and wind loads through variation of their stem sections and the organisation of their material in successive hierarchies, using small quantities of 'soft' materials in each organisational level to achieve their structural goals. Plants are hierarchical structures, made of materials with subtle properties that are capable of being changed by the plant in response to local or global stresses.

In classical engineering redundancy is opposed to efficiency, but it is an essential strategy for biology, without which adaptation and response to changing environmental pressures would not be possible. In biological systems, redundancy is the primary evolutionary strategy, therefore multicellular organisations developed from the seemingly very efficient unicellularity of primitive organisms. Cellular differentiation and multiple hierarchical arrangements of cells in which an aggregation of cells becomes a basic component in a higher organisational level add further complexity and increased functionality. Redundancy[3] in a biological structure means not only that the system has more cells available in each tissue than any single task would require, but also that the hierarchical organisation of cells is arranged so that tissue has sufficient excess capacity for adaptation to changing environmental stresses.

Evolutionary biology has utilised redundancy[4] as a deep strategy implemented at many levels, in multiple and complex hierarchical material arrangements and differentiation to achieve robust and stable structures, whereas engineering has traditionally sought the minimum of materials, simplicity of structural organisation, and the standardisation of components and members.

On the long timescale of evolution, the complexity of living systems, and the diversity of those systems, developed as responses to environmental pressures and instabilities. Those organisms that have excess capacities or redundancy survive environmental instability; those that are too completely matched to an environment – the 'efficient' design – do not survive if the environment develops instabilities. The most important principle of adaptation, unregarded by classical engineering, is small random variation in the 'design', repeated over time. It is this stochastic process that produces robust systems that persist through time. In mathematical terms, 'stochastic' is often used in opposition to the 'deterministic'. Deterministic processes always produce the same output from a given starting condition; stochastic processes will never repeat an identical output. It follows that developing processes that include small random mutations over many iterations is a significant 'evolutionary' strategy for design, architecture and engineering, and one that will preclude the standardisation of components and members.

During the self-assembly process of morphogenesis of an individual, the mutual interdependence of hierarchical levels of cellular organisation ensures that there is redundancy within each individual. The robust design of natural living systems is not produced by optimisation and standardisation, but by redundacy and differentiation.

In the sciences, the term 'robustness' is used to describe a system that can survive extreme external variations, and it is characteristic of a 'robust' system that it is not fatally sensitive to the variation of the inputs. Robustness[5] in living systems is produced at the genetic level. The genetic code can be described as canonical, persistent over enormous periods of time, but each time the code is transcribed to produce the amino acids that, in turn, self-organise into higher levels of assembly and differentiation, small copying errors produce sufficient mutation to ensure variation in the population. Each individual in the population will correspond to the main 'design parameters', being topologically identical, but individually varied. Furthermore, during the self-assembly process of morphogenesis of an individual, the mutual interdependence of hierarchical levels of cellular organisation ensures that there is redundancy within each individual. The robust design of natural living systems is not produced by optimisation and standardisation, but by redundancy and differentiation.

All biological forms assemble themselves, and do so under the load of gravity, when it is necessary to gather their

Three-dimensional models of the global morphology and internal fibre architecture of a bamboo stem. The global morphology model aims at accurately reproducing the geometry of the stem around the diaphragms and the internodal transition of the stem cross-section. The model of the internal fibre structure aims at reproducing the nonuniform fibre density across the stem's cross-section and the differentiation in the size and shape of the fibres.

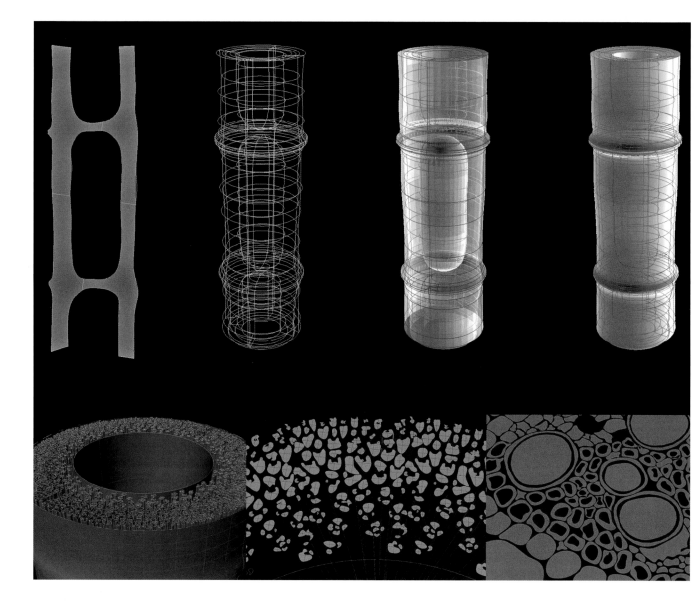

materials and energy from their environments. Biological self-organisation takes place under stress. If growth under stress is universal, it follows that geometrical morphologies and cellular organisations that allow plants to respond to stress loadings are also very common. Patterns appear in all natural systems, and the frequency and occurrence of certain geometrical patterns (in particular triangles, pentagons and spirals) in many different organisations and across hugely divergent scales is remarkable. These patterns are generic, and so it can be said that biological self-organisation is essentially geometrical, but it is also significant that the same small set of materials is common.

The critical characteristics of biological self-organisation are: small, simple components assembled together in three-dimensional patterns to form larger organisations that, in turn, self-assemble into more complex structures that have emergent properties and behaviour. An emergent property of human tissue, for example, is the mechanical behaviour of skin. Pinch an area of skin and pull, and the skin resists the force by becoming stiffer; let go and it relaxes. When skin is being stretched its resistance increases as the stress increases because more and more of the skin's components lie in the direction of the stress – a response to stress known as linear stiffening. Biological forms are systems within systems, hierarchical arrangements of semi-autonomous organisations,[6] each achieving its own functions, but also having sufficient excess capacity so that it contributes to the responsiveness of the global organisation. Each lower level of organisation requires differentiation and redundancy to achieve this.

The case for the evolutionary advantages conferred by differentiation and redundancy is convincing. However, there

Isosurfaces of the deformations occurring during tension loading of the bamboo stem, used for the study of the deformation patterns and stress trajectories around the internal diaphragms. Isosurfaces are algorithmically generated surfaces that cut through the stressed body so that they join the material points where equal deformations, strains or displacements develop.

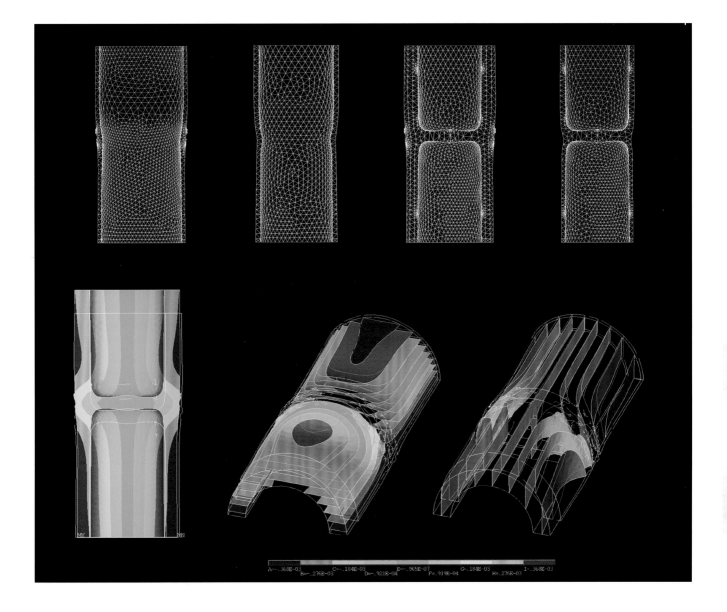

has yet to be any indepth study of the advantages to individuals as biological structures. The Emtech studies began with an examination of the integrated morphologies of plants, in search of potential systems from which innovative building systems can be developed. Quantitative descriptions and digital models are of value in understanding the structural performance of plants, and the construction of appropriate digital models enables analysis and simulations by experiment. The modelling and analysis of plant systems permits a new understanding of the emergent behaviour, component hierarchies and adaptive strategies of biological structures, and permits the exploration of the mechanical performance of growth under stress.

The investigation of plant systems commenced with a preliminary phase of case studies of bamboos and palms. The digital modelling and analysis was conducted within the Emtech Masters programme at the Architectural Association (AA), with the assistance of George Jeronimidis and Nikolaos Stathopoulos. It immediately became evident that there are strategic decisions to be made in developing digital models for analysis. Models are needed in order to explore the relationship of global morphology to tissue mechanics, but if every cell in a plant system is modelled, the computational resources that would be required would be immense.[7] Digital modelling of plant systems also introduces many other complications. Not only are the geometry, boundary and loading conditions difficult to define accurately, but it is also necessary to define the characteristics of 'biological' materials. Therefore, in order to analyse the mechanical behaviour and to reveal how cell tissues, leaves and stems respond to externally applied loads and localised stresses, we developed digital models in a hierarchical manner.

Numerical methods and, particularly, the finite element approach, are now increasingly common in the study of biological systems. Finite element analysis (FEA) is now a well-known technique for the analysis of manufactured engineering structures, familiar to engineers and to many architects. The finite element method is a numerical analysis technique used to obtain solutions to the differential equations that are used to describe a wide variety of physical problems. A geometrical model consisting of multiple, linked, simplified representations of discrete components – the finite elements – represents the material system. Data transfer between typical 3-D modelling software programs and analytical software creates particular difficulties, and requires the development of specific protocols.

The inherent problem in breaking down a complex natural system into hierarchies and components is that emergent behaviour produced by the interdependence of different hierarchical levels can only be described in a simplistic manner. Associative modelling, such as that offered by the GenerativeComponents software (Bentley Systems), is an effective way to link material systems in layered hierarchies, and coupling that, in turn, to analytical software for behavioural analysis will be the focus of subsequent inquiries.

Bamboo

Bamboo occurs in natural environments with varying stem diameters and a range of heights. Unlike trees, the anatomical features and mechanical behaviour of bamboo exhibit no really significant differences across the 1200 or so different species. Growth conditions and the age of individual plants do not appear to have a significant effect on the anatomy or on the material composition of the tissue in the stem.

Again unlike trees, the growth is mainly longitudinal, with proportionally little radial growth. The stem (or 'culm') is made up of approximately 50 per cent long cylindrical cells (parenchyma), 40 per cent fibres and 10 per cent xylem, or hollow fluid-conducting tubes, which have fibres arranged in sheaths and bundles around them.[8] All bamboos show a marked differentiation in the distribution of cells within the stem, both horizontally and vertically. The percentage of fibres is much higher in the outer third of the wall than in the inner, and in the upper part of the stem compared to the lower part. The distribution of fibres and bundles is differentiated according to height and slenderness, so that the upper parts of the stem consist mainly of many smaller vascular bundles with a higher portion of fibres, ensuring that, as the slenderness increases, so too does the material strength increase appropriately to the increased loading stresses of wind and water on the higher parts of the plant.

This fibre and bundle differentiation offers a very interesting model for the production of fibre-composite materials systems, which currently tend towards a uniform distribution of fibres and matrix (carbon-fibre materials and glass-fibre-reinforced materials are commonly produced in this way). Thus differentiation offers the potential for variable stiffness and elasticity within the same material.

We employed associative modelling software[9] (the beta GenerativeComponents)[10] to establish a relation between the various 'components' of the bamboo, a relation controlled by a global variable in the digital model. When the height of the stem was increased in the model, the width of the stem reduced, simulating the natural growth pattern. This relationship was then extrapolated to the model of the whole bamboo, and used to simulate its structural response to a variety of dynamic load conditions.

The aim was to construct a digital model that linked the plant's global morphology (its general form) and anatomy (its internal structure), so that geometric studies such as curvature analysis, and structural studies such as deflection analysis, could be carried out. The structural behaviour at various scales was tested, from the stem and root of the bamboo down to its microscopic fibrous structure. The initial research focused on establishing scale relations between these 'components', and the digital model was developed according to this logic. The relative densities and strengths of materials (the fibres and surrounding matrix) were established, so that simulations of the response to various stresses and loadings could be carried out using the FEA software Ansys.

Bamboo can grow to heights of up to 30 metres (98 feet). Though it has a very thin section, it does not buckle as it

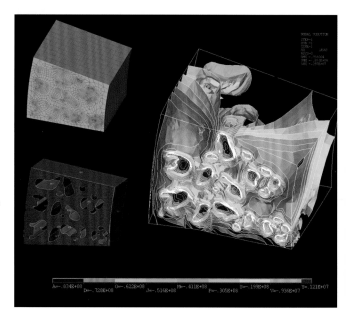

Isosurfaces of stresses along the main direction of the fibres when a sector of the bamboo stem is subjected to tension. The visualisation facilitates a quick reading of the interaction between the stiff fibres and the much softer surrounding material matrix.

sways in the wind. The simulations and analysis demonstrated that bamboo negotiates stresses far more efficiently than manmade structures, and does so with a minimum of material. Bamboo is an extremely strong fibre, with twice the compressive strength of concrete and roughly the same strength-to-weight ratio of steel in tension. The tests demonstrated that the hollow-cylinder configuration gives a strength factor of 1.9 over an equivalent solid when used as a beam, as in a beam only the top (compression) and bottom (tension) are doing any work – the material in the centre does no work and only adds weight. The internal diaphragms reduce the effective length of the bamboo relative to the section, so that each internodal length of stem is quite stiff (short length in relation to diameter), yet the global geometry produces flexibility (very long in relation to stem diameter). The variation, or differentiation, of the internode dimensions along the length of the stem produces a graduated response to dynamic loadings and the ability to tolerate bending deflections.

If these naturally occurring material strategies are described in engineering terms, there is an agenda for new strategies for design, including differentiated distribution of cells, bundles and fibres in a bamboo section to produce anisotropic and emergent structural properties, shape adaptation at nodes, variable sections and differentiated component dimensions (diaphragms) along the length of the member.

Palms

Palm trees show a comparable strategy to bamboo in the density and distribution of materials in the stem, and the anatomy of palms[11] is quite different again from that of trees. The palm stem is strongly differentiated, with more marked internal differences. Within the stem, density of fibrous bundles is highest towards the outer part of the stem and lower at the centre, and much higher at the base than at the crown. A single palm can demonstrate the full range of densities found in all trees – the density of the peripheral stem tissues at the base of a palm is greater than that of most woods, while the less dense core tissue near the crown is lower. The material differentiation and changing stem diameter (or allometry) along the length are responsible for the very high capacity of the palm to respond to exceptional dynamic loading.

The folded structure and overall contoured shape of the palm leaf assist in maximising collection of both water and sunlight, and contribute to the strength and stability of the leaf. Study and analysis here focused on the global morphology of the leaf and the structural articulations of the folds, and the morphology of the stem. In the simulations of loadings and subsequent analysis, the stresses on the lower edges of the folds were highest, precisely corresponding with distribution of the veins that provide additional stiffening as well as fulfilling their primary role in the management of fluids.

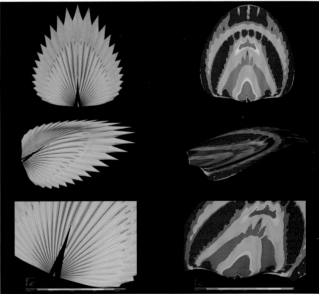

Study of the structural performance of a folded-plate palm leaf structure by means of comparing the stress patterns developing over the leaf due to wind pressures with the stresses that would develop over a leaf with similar global geometry but no folds.

The joint between the leaf and the stem of the palm raised a problem common in all our studies. Unlike engineered structures, in natural biological systems there is no single boundary or contour where one component ends and the other begins; fibrous material is continuous right through the joint. In fact, in plants there do not seem to be any joints at all, thus the zone where the palm leaf joins its stem has to be defined as a morphological change rather than a mechanical change. The main leaf stem has a particular moon-shaped cross-section that continuously changes along the length from the lower stem to the base of the leaf.

The stem allotropy (stem diameter in relation to tree height) demonstrates another variation on a similar strategy found in the bamboo, in that a variable section produces anisotropic properties, and a gradation of values between stiffness and elasticity along the length of the stem that is particularly useful for resisting dynamic and unpredictable loadings. All the stems come together towards the base of the plant, and this collective grouping acts as a bundle to assist in strength stability and bending stiffness of the whole plant.

Nonlinear Dynamics

The preliminary studies of plant morphologies and anatomy described above focus on linear dynamics, even though it is evident that most biological materials have marked stiffness nonlinearities. The range of their elastic behaviour, their ability to accept large stresses and deformations and return to their previous state, is far higher than is the case with engineered structures. Plants can accept very high temporary loadings, and even in high gusting winds and severe storms it is more common for palms and bamboo to be uprooted than it is for their stems to snap. Of particular interest is the way in which these plant systems deal with resonance, a phenomena that is critical to the design of tall structures, and perhaps more familiarly, to spanning structures and bridges.

All structures vibrate at a frequency that is unique to the structure, and resonance can be thought of as a vibration that is caused by the tendency of the system to absorb energy from an external force that is in harmony with the natural frequency of the structure itself. Musical instruments are designed and built on this principle, so that the acoustic resonances of the instrument produce musical harmonies. All natural structures, and most engineered structures, have more than one resonant frequency, and will vibrate more easily in some frequencies than in others. Resonance is nonlinear, but in certain circumstances the resonant frequency will emerge from a complex 'excitation', such as wind. If it is not dampened, this can lead to catastrophic failure, perhaps the most famous example of which is the oscillations that destroyed the Tacoma Narrows Suspension Bridge in 1940. The wind was not severe, perhaps just 68 kilometres (42 miles) per hour, but was at the precise speed

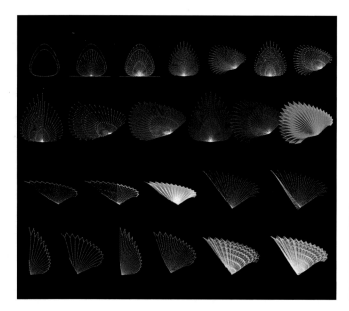

Successive generations of NURBS-Surface models of the 3-D folded-plate geometry of the palm leaf. The models explore different strategies for the geometric modelling of the folded structure and their repercussions for the subsequent transfer of geometrical data to engineering finite element analysis software.

Analysis of the bending stresses developing at different sections of the palm stem. The cross-section is continuously changing along the stem's length, leading to different local bending stress distributions at different sections and contributing to a global relationship between bending and torsional stiffness that is not possible with a constant cross-section.

and the correct angle to start the bridge vibrating. The vibrations continued to accelerate, the energy being supplied by the wind, until the waves travelling through the structure broke the bridge apart. There was no significant damping in the structural design to prevent the torsional fluttering that caused the destruction.

A related example is the Millennium Bridge (AKA the 'wobbly bridge' across the Thames, the 'blade of light' design by Arup and Foster and Partners). Here, the suspension cables are below the pedestrian deck level, giving a very shallow profile, but analysis has shown that it was not the shallowness of the profile, but rather the movement of pedestrians walking in synchronisation, that caused the unexpected lateral vibration or resonance. This resonance was not anticipated in the computational analysis at the design stage, and was 'cured' only later on by the fitting of 37 fluid-viscous dampers to control the horizontal movements and 52 tuned mass dampers to control the vertical movements.

The variable stiffness of plants means they behave very differently in resonance than linear models of conventional structural dynamics. Although yet to be confirmed by more detailed analysis and simulation, it is clear that the ways in which bamboos and palms cope with resonance is by 'torsional softness', a way of transferring bending energy into twisting energy. The shape variation of the stem section means that mass distribution along the stem is asymmetrical, and as the fibre density is also varied the elastic modulus of the stem has a gradation of values rather than a uniform condition. This means that twisting and bending are coupled, a significant engineering advantage for the resonant behaviour of the plant. Plant stems can thus behave somewhat like springs of variable 'softness', so that their response is tuned to the strain imposed on them.

Conclusion: Redundancy and Differentiation

The structural dynamics of all natural systems are complex and adaptive, and plants in particular manage their structural behaviour in a way that provides new models for engineered structures. It is clear that plant systems offer a model of structure and material organisation that presents considerable challenges to traditional engineering concepts. 'Efficiency' and 'optimisation' have very different meanings in biological structures, which feature a high degree of redundancy and complexity in their material hierarchies. The means by which biological systems respond and adapt to environmental stresses and dynamic loadings are complex, so that responses are nonlinear, arising out of the interactions of multiple material hierarchies. The high performance that shape-adaptation at nodes and continuity of materials in biological structures produces suggests that the mechanical joint in engineered structures needs to be rethought and, if possible, eliminated.

Variations in the section and material properties of biological 'structural members' offer very considerable advantages over the constant section usually adopted in conventional engineered structures. The differentiated distribution of cells, fibres and bundles, according to height and slenderness, offers a very interesting model for the production of fibre-composite materials systems. Sectional variations produce anisotropy, a gradation of values between stiffness and elasticity along the length of the stem that is particularly useful for resisting dynamic and unpredictable loadings. ⌂

Notes

1. An introduction to some aspects of dynamics in biological systems is presented by Professor George Jeronimidis in 'Biodynamics', ⌂ *Emergence: Morphogenetic Design Strategies*, Vol 74, No 3, 2004.
2. M Elices (ed), *Structural Biological Materials*, Pergamon Press (Amsterdam), 2000. An excellent study of the structure and properties of biological materials, including hard and soft tissue engineering, and fibrous materials.
3. In many biological systems, the ability of elements that are structurally different but can perform the same function is known as 'degeneracy', and it is argued that this property is a significant characteristic of systems such as genes, neural networks and evolution itself. Degeneracy is distinguished from 'redundancy', which occurs when the same function is performed by identical elements. See Guilo Tononi, Olaf Sporns and Gerald M Edelman, 'Measures of degeneracy and redundancy in biological networks', *Proceedings of the National Academy of Science USA*, Vol 98, Issue 6, 3257–3262, 1999. See also Gerald M Edelman and Joseph A Gally, 'Degeneracy and complexity in biological systems', *Proceedings of the National Academy of Science USA*, Vol 98, Issue 6, 13763–13768, 2001.
4. Evolvability is an organism's capacity to generate heritable phenotypic variation, and it is argued that the various controlling processes of evolutionary change include redundancy. This contributes to robustness and flexibility of processes during individual embryonic development, and also confers evolvability on the organism by reducing constraints on change and allowing the accumulation of beneficial variations. See Marc Kirschner and John Gerhart, 'Evolvability', *Proceedings of the National Academy of Science USA*, Vol 95, Issue 15, 8420–8427, 1998.
5. David C Krakauer, 'Robustness in biological systems: a provisional taxonomy', Sante Fe Institute Paper 03-02-008, USA, 2003; and Andreas Wagner, *Robustness and Evolvability in Living Systems*, Princeton University Press (Princeton, NJ), 2005.
6. HA Simon, 'The architecture of complexity', *Proceedings of the American Philosophical Society* 106, in *The Sciences of the Artificial*, 3rd edn, MIT Press (Cambridge, MA), 1996.
7. David M Bruce, 'Mathematical modelling of the cellular mechanics of plants', *Philosophical Transactions of the Royal Society of London*, Vol 358, No 1437, September 2003. 'The complex mechanical behaviour of plant tissues reflects the complexity of their structure and material properties. This paper reviews approaches that have been taken to modelling and simulation of cell wall, cell and tissue mechanics, and to what extent models have been successful in predicting mechanical behaviour.'
8. Christina Sanchis Gritch and Richard J Murphy, 'Ultrastructure of fibre and parenchyma cell walls during culm development in *Dendrocalamus asper*', *Annals of Botany 2005*, 95: 619–29.
9. Associative modelling allows the linking of geometrically defined objects to each other and in cascading multiple hierarchies. Any local changes to the geometry of a single object will then be automatically implemented to all linked objects and assemblies.
10. Bentley Systems' GenerativeComponents is a parametric and associative design system. It gives designers and engineers new ways to efficiently explore alternative building forms without manually building the detail design model for each scenario.
11. Rodolfo Salm, 'Stem density, growth and the distribution of palm trees', *Biota Neotropica*, Vol 4, 2004.

Self-Organisation and Material Constructions

Cellular biological materials have intricate interior structures, self-organised in hierarchies to produce modularity, redundancy and differentiation. As **Michael Weinstock** explains, the foam geometries of cellular materials offer open and ductile structural systems that are strong and permeable, making them an attractive paradigm for developments in material science and for new structural systems in architecture and engineering.

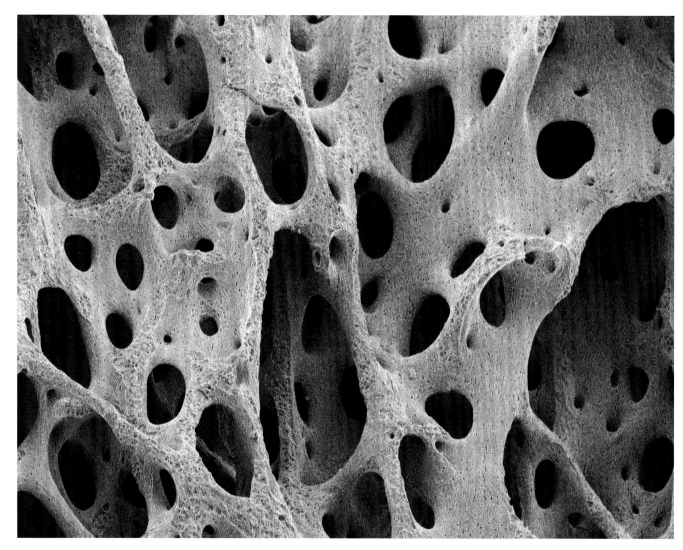

Spongy bone tissue
Scanning electron micrograph of cancellous (spongy) bone tissue. Bone can be either cortical (compact solid) or cancellous, with cortical usually forming the exterior of the bone and cancellous tissue forming the interior. The cellular structure is highly differentiated, formed by an irregular network of trabeculae, or rod-shaped fibrous tissue. The open spaces within the tissue are filled with bone marrow.

In recent years, new strategies for design and new techniques for making materials and large constructions have emerged, based on biological models of the processes by which natural material forms are produced. Biological organisms have evolved multiple variations of form that should not be thought of as separate from their structure and materials. Such a distinction is artificial, in view of the complex hierarchies within natural structures and the emergent properties of assemblies. Form, structure and material act upon each other, and this behaviour of all three cannot be predicted by analysis of any one of them separately.

The self-organisation of biological material systems is a process that occurs over time, a dynamic that produces the capacity for changes to the order and structure of a system, and for those changes to modify the behaviour of that system.[1] The characteristics of self-organisation include a 3-D spatial structure, redundancy and differentiation, hierarchy and modularity.[2] Studies of biological systemic development suggest that the critical factor is the spontaneous emergence of several distinct organisational scales and the interrelations between lower or local levels of organisation, the molecular and cellular level, and higher or global levels of the structure or organism as a whole. The evolution and development of biological self-organisation of systems proceeds from small, simple components that are assembled together to form larger structures that have emergent properties and behaviour, which, in turn, self-assemble into more complex structures.[3] The geometry of soap foams is a model for the cellular arrangements at all scales in natural physical systems.

Natural Constructions

Natural materials develop under load, and the intricate interior structure of biological materials is an evolutionary response. At the level of the individual, there is also an adaptive response as, for example, bone tissue gets denser in response to repeated loads in athletic activities such as weightlifting. Bone is a cellular solid,[4] a porous material that has the appearance of mineralised foam, and its interior is a network of very small and intricately connected structures. When bone becomes less dense, due to age or prolonged inactivity, it is the very small connective material that vanishes, so that the spaces or cells within the bone become larger. The loss of strength in the material is disproportionate, demonstrating the importance of the microstructure: larger cells make a weaker material.

Cellular materials are common at many scales in the natural world, for example in the structure of tiny sea creatures, in wood and in bones. What they have in common is an internal structure of 'cells', voids or spaces filled with air or fluids, each of which has edges and faces of liquid or solid material. The cells are polyhedral, and pack all the available arranged space in a 3-D pattern. Foam has cells that are differentially organised in space, whereas honeycombs are organised in parallel rows and tend to have more regular, prism-like cells. In all cellular materials, the cells may be either regular or irregular shapes, and may vary in distribution.

D'Arcy Thompson[5] discussed the mathematical expressions for the shapes of growing cells in 1917, arguing that new biological structures arise because of the mathematical and physical properties of living matter. His chapter on 'The Forms of Cells', when read in conjunction with the 'Theory of Transformations', has been extended today to patterning and differentiation in plant morphogenesis. The problem of mathematical descriptions of foam has a long history,[6] but it can be observed that foam will comprise a randomised array of hexagon and pentagon structures.[7] Diatoms and radiolara are among the smallest of sea creatures, and the intricate structures of their skeletons have fascinated, among others, Frei Otto and his biologist collaborator JG Helmke. It has been argued that the formation of these tiny intricate structures is a process of mineralised deposits on the intersection surfaces of aggregations of pneus or bubbles.

The Construction of Materials

In the industrial world, polymer cellular foams[8] are widely used for insulation and packaging, but the high structural efficiency of cellular materials in other, stiffer materials has only recently begun to be explored. Comparatively few engineers and architects are familiar with the engineering design of cellular materials, and this has contributed to the slow development of cellular structures in architecture.

Industrial and economic techniques do exist for producing foams in metals, ceramics and glass. Foamed cellular materials take advantage of the unique combination of properties offered by cellular solids, analogous properties to those of biological materials, but they do not share their origin. They are structured and manufactured in ways that are derived from biological materials, but are made from inorganic matter. The production processes for metal foams and cellular ceramics have been developed for the simultaneous optimisation of stiffness and permeability, strength and low overall weight. This is the logic of biomimesis, abstracting principles from the way in which biological processes develop a natural material system, applying analogous methods in an industrial context, and using stronger materials to manufacture a material that has no natural analogue.

The ability of some materials to self-organise into a stable arrangement under stress has been the founding principle of structural form-finding in the physical experiments of Gaudí Eisler and Otto. 'Organisation' here refers to the reordering of the material, or the components of the material system, in order to produce structural stability.

Biomimetics is essentially interdisciplinary, a series of collaborations and exchanges between mathematicians,

Soap bubbles
A naturally produced foam of soap bubbles, demonstrating the differentiation of polyhedral cells in an intricate geometry of foam architecture, including the basic Plateau rules for the intersection of three films.

Polyurethane foam wound dressing
Scanning electron micrograph of polyurethane foam, showing the porous structure of differentiated open and partially closed cells. Magnification x 20 when printed at 10 centimetres wide.

physicists, engineers, botanists, doctors and zoologists. The rigid boundaries between the inherited taxonomy of 'pure' disciplines make little sense in this new territory. Similarly, the traditional architectural and engineering ways of thinking about materials as something independent of form and structure are obsolete.

New research into the molecular assembly of structures and materials in what were previously thought to be homogenous natural materials has led to 'biomimetic' manufacturing techniques for producing synthetic materials, and new composite materials are being 'grown' that have increasingly complex internal structures based on biological models. The fabrication of composites relies on controlling structure internal to the material itself, at molecular levels. Here, processing is the controlling parameter and growth is more than a metaphor. 'Grown' materials are layered, molecule by molecule, to create distinctive micro-structures in thin films, making new combinations of metal and ceramic that are produced by design rather than 'nature'. New composites such as flaw-tolerant ceramics and directionally solidified metals might seem to be a long way from the materials available to architects, but they are already in use in many other fields.

Other 'designed' materials, such as polymers and foamed metals, are already being used in many aerospace, maritime and medical applications. Polymers also have unique combinations of properties not found in 'natural' materials, being lightweight, very flexible and mechanically strong. In tandem with their electrical and optical properties, this makes them highly suited to military applications. In aircraft fuselages and body armour they offer high strength for low weight, providing structural stability and flexibility.

Simple polymers, such as the ubiquitous plastics like DuPont's Corian, are homogenous materials, similar in density and strength in all directions. Complex polymers need not be homogenous, and can be produced with surfaces that have different properties from the polymer interior. Complex polymers are useful for films and surfaces with multiple layers, each with distinct and differentiated functions. Manufactured by mimicking and adapting the self-organising behaviour and complex functions of natural polymers, very strong transparent or translucent films can be produced with a water-repellent and self-cleaning surface for facade systems. The process, known as 'free living radical polymerisation', can produce honeycomb structures at a molecular level, although the controlled formation of the honeycomb morphology at larger scales is still

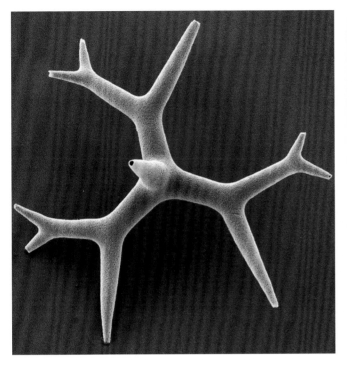

Sponge spicule
Scanning electron micrograph of the endoskeletal component of a sponge made of calcium carbonate. When assembled, the skeleton forms either a mesh or honeycomb structure. Magnification x 210 when printed at 10 centimetres wide.

The process, known as 'free living radical polymerisation', can produce honeycomb structures at a molecular level, although the controlled formation of the honeycomb morphology at larger scales is still in the research, rather than production, phase.

Thomas Von Girsewald and Juan Subercaseaux, centroidal Voronoi tessellation and boundary optimisation in close-packing systems, Emergent Technologies and Design programme, AA Graduate School of Architecture, 2005
Geometric logics were identified from a physical soap-film model and, based on the geometric fundamentals of Plateau's laws extended into three dimensions (three relaxed soap bubbles can only meet at an angle of exactly 109° 28' 16"), a four-segment tetrahedral dihedral angle component was digitally designed. The component was nested inside a layered triangular organisation generating a parametrically deformable triangular tile with regular pentagonal dodecahedra (12-sided) interior cellular partitions. This tile was aperiodically distributed into a larger equilateral configuration with a total population of 152 nested component features. The parametric system permits the manipulation of one single input point to produce an automatic reconfiguration of 114 primary components, maintaining the coherence of the cellular partitions while relocating the respected individual centroid.

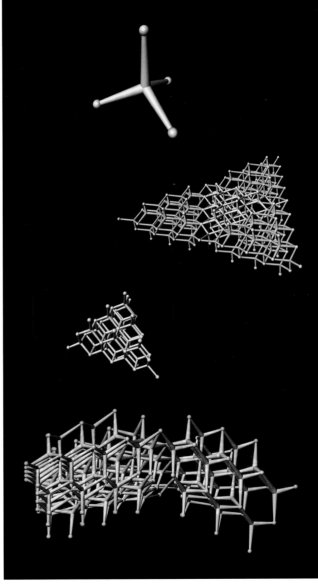

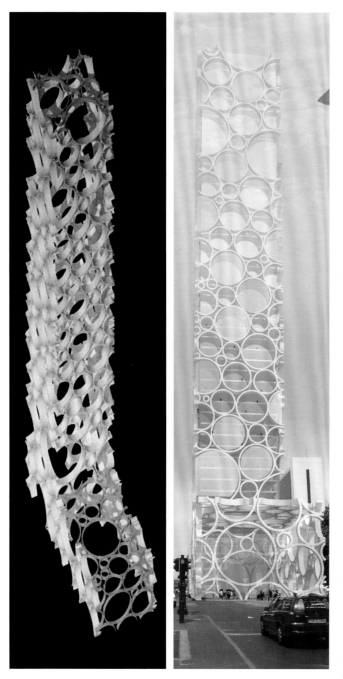

SMO Architektur and Arup, Bubble Highrise, Berlin, 2002
Experimental design from which the design approach to the Watercube was evolved. The structure is produced by running a packing algorithm to fill a notional high-rise volume with differentiated spheres, which are then cut at the surface intersection.

in the research, rather than production, phase.

Kevlar is perhaps the best-known manufactured organic fibre and, because of its unique combination of material properties, it is now widely used in many industrial applications. It has high tensile strength (five times that of steel), low weight and excellent dimensional stability, and so has been adopted for lightweight cables and ropes in many marine and naval applications. Kevlar has high impact resistance, so it is the major fibre constituent in composite panels in military and civil aircraft, and in sporting equipment such as canoes, skis, racquets and helmets. However, it has yet to be used widely in architectural construction.

Liquid crystals have the flow properties of a conventional liquid, and the molecular structure of a solid crystal. This is a phase change occurring between the crystalline and isotropic liquid states. Kevlar is produced, in part, by manipulating the liquid-crystalline state in polymers. Spiders use the low viscosity in the liquid crystalline regime for the spinning of their silk. Spider silk is as strong as Kevlar, which means that it has superior mechanical properties to most synthetic fibres and can stretch up to 40 per cent under load. This gives it an unusual advantage, in that the amount of strain required to cause failure actually increases as deformation increases, an energy-absorbing ability that allows the web to absorb the impact of flying prey.

Self-organising materials, such as liquid crystals, natural polymers and copolymers, found their first applications in biotechnology, sensor development and smart medical surfaces, and more recently in maritime, automotive and aerospace applications, but they have the potential to produce new structures and systems for advanced architectural engineering.

There is new interest within the material sciences and industry in the use of ceramics as a structural material. Ceramics are very light, but their compressive strength matches, or exceeds, that of metals. They are hard and durable, resistant to abrasion and noncorroding as they are chemically inert. Ceramics are good insulators (both electric and thermal) and can resist high temperatures. However, they have one major disadvantage: their lack of tensile strength. The solution to this problem is being sought in biological models – the forming of complex structures internal to the material – and as new production facilities come online ceramics may become the most ubiquitous of new materials for built structures. Cellular ceramics are porous and can now be manufactured in various morphologies and topologies, ranging from honeycombs and foams to structures woven from fibres, rods and hollow spheres. Substitutes for human bone and the coating of orthopaedic prostheses are produced by similar methods.

Injecting a stream of gas bubbles into liquid metals is the basic technique for producing foamed metals, but preventing

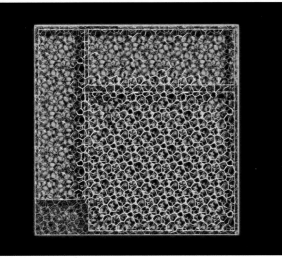

PTW **Architects,** CSCEG **Design and Arup, 'Watercube' National Swimming Centre, Beijing, due for completion 2007**
Competition model showing overall scale: 177 x 177 metres (581 x 581 feet) and more than 30 metres (98 feet) high, with an entirely column-free interior space.

Watercube digital structural model. The mathematics of foam geometries are used to produce the structural array, ensuring a rational optimised and buildable structural geometry.

the bubbles from collapsing is difficult. Adding a small quantity of insoluble particles to slow the flow of the liquid metal stabilises the bubbles in the production of aluminium foam sheets, produced with open or closed cells on the surface. Aluminium foams can be cast in complex 3-D forms, are stronger and more rigid than polymer foams, can tolerate relatively high temperatures, and are recyclable and stable over time. They are very light, nominally about 10 per cent of the density of the metal, and are currently used as a structural reinforcement material, particularly in aerospace applications, though they have not yet reached their full potential in lightweight architectural structures.

Closed-cell aluminium honeycomb is widely used as the core material of panel structures, conventionally with other materials as a surface. This is no longer strictly necessary, as new advanced processes produce 'self-finished' surfaces of high quality. Cellular metals including, but not exclusively, aluminium, are being deployed for applications such as acoustic absorption, vibration damping and innovative thermal regulation. As the frequency and range of applications increases, data accumulates for the relationship between the topology of cells in the foam and the subsequent performance of the cellular material, so that improved and optimised cell topologies can be produced.

Another new open-cell foamed material, made of a glass-like carbon combining properties of glass and industrial carbons,

can be used for biological 'scaffolding'. Reticulated vitreous carbon has a large surface area combined with a very high percentage of void spaces, is sufficiently rigid to be self-supporting, and is biologically and chemically inert. Cellular glass structures are used in medical applications for bone regeneration. The bioactive glass acts as a scaffold to guide the growth and differentiation of new cells, and this requires an open-cell structure that is highly interconnected at the nanometre scale. The cells must be large enough to allow the bone tissue to grow between the cells, yet fine enough so that the 'bioglass' material can be absorbed into the bone as it is replaced by living tissue.

Material Constructions

Design and construction strategies based on space-filling polyhedra and foam geometries offer open structural systems that are robust and ductile. Control of the cell size, the distribution and differentiation of sizes within the global structure and the degree and number of connections are variables that can be explored to produce strength and permeability. SMO Architektur and Arup designed the Bubble Highrise by packing a notional structural volume with bubbles of various sizes, then used the intersection of the bubbles and the exterior planes of the notional volume to generate a structure that gives entirely column-free interior spaces. The 'Watercube' National Swimming Centre, Beijing, to be finished in 2007, was

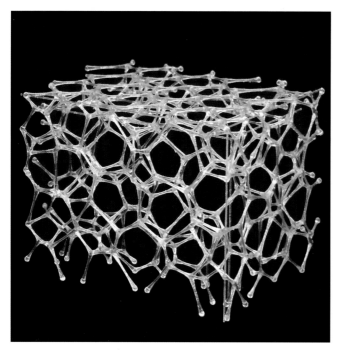

Watercube resin model.

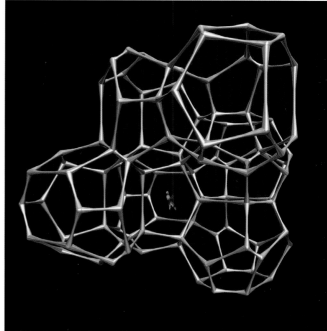

Watercube digital model of cell cluster.

designed by PTW Architects and Arup using a structural design developed from Weaire and Phelan's soap bubbles arrays. Despite the appearance of randomness, the elements of the structure are highly rational and so economically buildable. The Watercube is an enormous building, 177 metres (581 feet) on each side and more than 30 metres (98 feet) high. The network of steel tubular members is clad with translucent ETFE pillows. Over such a wide span of column-free space, the need to minimise the self-weight of the structure is paramount, as most of the structural work involves ensuring the roof can hold itself up.

The steel tubes are welded to round steel nodes that vary according to the loads placed upon them. There is a substantial variation in size, with a total of around 22,000 steel members and 12,000 nodes.

There is a total of 4000 'bubbles' in the Watercube, the roof being made of only 7 variant types (of bubbles) and the walls of only 16 variations, which are repeated throughout. The geometry was developed by extensive scripting, using the Weaire and Phelan mathematics, with a further script required for a final analytical and geometrical correct 3-D model. Scripts that run in minutes can deal with the tens of thousands of nodes and beam elements, and scripting was also used to develop structural analysis models and models from which drawings were automatically generated.

The ETFE cushions make the building very energy efficient, and sufficient solar energy is trapped within to heat the pools and the interior area, with daylight maximised throughout the interior spaces.

Conclusion

A systematic change is on the horizon, whereby the boundary between the 'natural' and the 'manufactured' will no longer exist. The complex interaction between form, material and structure of natural material systems has informed new 'biomimetic' industrial processes, generating new high-performance materials. New processes are having a compelling impact on many industries, and new materials are radically transforming aerospace and maritime design and medicine. Cellular materials, especially metals and ceramics, offer an entirely new set of performance and material values, and have the potential to reinform and revitalise the material strategies of architectural engineering and construction.

At the scale of very large architectural projects, the emphasis on process becomes not only the significant design strategy, but also the only economic means of reducing design data for manufacturing. Biomimetic strategies that integrate form, material and structure into a single process are being adopted from the nanoscale right up to the design and construction of very large buildings. ⋈

Watercube physical prototype; cells and ETFE cushions fabricated for the testing of environmental and structural behaviour, and confirmation of production logics.

Notes
1. Stuart A Kauffman, *The Origins of Order: Self-Organization and Selection in Evolution*, Oxford University Press (Oxford), 1993.
2. 'A combination of emergence and self-organisation is often present in complex dynamical systems. In such systems, the complexity is huge, which makes it infeasible to impose a structure a priori: the system needs to self-organise. Also, the huge number of individual entities imposes a need for emergence.' Tom De Wolf and Tom Holvoet, 'Emergence and self-organisation: a statement of similarities and differences', *Proceedings of the International Workshop on Engineering Self-Organising Applications 2004*, Belgium.
3. Francis Heylighen, 'Self-organisation, emergence and the architecture of complexity', *Proceedings of the 1st European Conference on System Science*, 1989.
4. The structure and properties of cellular solids such as engineering honeycombs, foams, wood, cancellous bone and cork have similarities of behaviour and can be exploited for engineering design. Case studies show how the models for foam behaviour can be used in the selection of the optimum foam for a particular engineering application. See LJ Gibson and MF Ashby, *Cellular Solids: Structure and Properties*, Cambridge University Press (Cambridge), 1997.
5. D'Arcy Thompson, *On Growth and Form*, Cambridge University Press (Cambridge), 1961, first published 1917.
6. Plateau's observation in 1873 that when soap films come together, they do so as three surfaces meeting at 120 degrees, and Lord Kelvin's 1883 challenge of subdividing a 3-D space into multiple compartments or cells.
7. D Weaire and R Phelan, 'A counterexample to Kelvin's conjecture on minimal surfaces', *Philosophical Magazine Letters*, Vol 69, 1994. See also D Weaire, 'Froths, foams and heady geometry', *New Scientist*, 21 May 1994.
8. Denis Weaire and Stefan Hutzler, *The Physics of Foams*, Oxford University Press (Oxford), 2001.

**Foster and Partners, Smithsonian Institute Courtyard
Enclosure, Washington** DC**, 2004**
Courtyard enclosure roof structure.

Instrumental Geometry

For two decades, the individual members of the SmartGeometry Group have pioneered innovative computer-aided design (CAD) techniques and technologies. Now that they are situated in key positions in internationally renowned companies, the group is involved in developing a new generation of parametric design software. Here, Robert Aish (Director of Research at Bentley Systems), Lars Hesselgren (Director of Research and Development, KPF London), J Parrish (Director of ArupSport) and Hugh Whitehead (Project Director of the Specialist Modelling Group, Foster and Partners, London) discuss with **Achim Menges** the group's instrumental approach to geometry and their unique collaboration spanning the world of practice and software development.

Geometry has always played a central role in architectural discourse. In recent years, the importance of geometry has been re-emphasised by significant advances in computer-aided design (CAD) and the advent of digital fabrication and performance analysis methods. New design approaches are being developed that will profoundly change the current nature and established hierarchies of architectural practice. The arrival of parametric digital modelling changes digital representations of architectural design from explicit geometric notation to instrumental geometric relationships. Architects are beginning to shift away from primarily designing the specific shape of a building to setting up geometric relationships and principles described through parametric equations that can derive particular design instances as a response to specific variables, expressions, conditional statements and scripts.

Robert Aish, Lars Hesselgren, J Parrish and Hugh Whitehead have been at the forefront of these developments for many years. The formative period for their collaboration, when the intent and methodology of parametric design applied to architecture was established, was the time when all of them were working for, or in collaboration with, YRM in the mid-1980s. There they took Integraph's Vehicle Design System and applied it to pioneering buildings such as the Grimshaw Waterloo International Rail Terminal and the 'Stadium for the Nineties', a project that featured a retractable roof defined through fully associative geometry. Since then, Robert Aish has moved on to become Director of Research at Bentley Systems, where he is responsible for the development of new parametric design software. Lars Hesselgren is Director of

Research and Development at KPF London, where he has been involved with many major building projects, most recently the Bishopsgate Tower. Hugh Whitehead leads the Specialist Modelling Group at Foster and Partners that has provided consultancy on such prominent buildings as the Swiss Re Tower, GLA City Hall, the Sage Gateshead and Beijing airport. J Parrish, Director of ArupSport, has contributed to the development of outstanding sports stadiums such as the Sydney Olympic Stadium and the Allianz Arena in Munich. Together they formed the SmartGeometry Group, and here they outline their common views on the aim of the group.

'The objective of the SmartGeometry Group,' says Lars Hesselgren, 'is to create the intellectual foundations for a more profound way of designing. Change can only be additive, not subtractive, so SmartGeometry does not reject or deny existing, more informal or intuitive approaches to design. What SmartGeometry initially set out to achieve was to add to the established skills other complementary formal systems of notation that would allow for the creation and control of more complex geometry. We recognised that architecture, and design in the broadest sense, was critically dependent on geometry, but that a complete geometric tradition of the understanding of descriptive and construct geometry was being lost through lack of use in a bland planar and orthogonal minimalism or, indeed, through misuse by being excessively indulged at the "hyper" fringes of design. Against

'The objective of the SmartGeometry Group was to reassert an understanding of geometry in design as more than an "experiential commodity". Rather than being wilful and arbitrary, even the most complex geometry could provide a formal resolution of competing forces and requirements. It could suggest and resolve both structural efficiency and environmental sensitivity.'

this background, the objective of the SmartGeometry Group was to reassert an understanding of geometry in design as more than an "experiential commodity". Rather than being wilful and arbitrary, even the most complex geometry could provide a formal resolution of competing forces and requirements. It could suggest and resolve both structural efficiency and environmental sensitivity.'

He summarises the group's active engagement in building up new skills and techniques for current and future generations of architects: 'The group aims to help create the intellectual environment for further developments in this field that stretch beyond relatively simple geometric mechanisms into more complex approaches to the generation and evaluation of built forms.'

In pursuing an instrumental understanding of geometry, the group identified very early on the limits of 'conventional' CAD concepts that mimic pen and paper with mouse and screen, and constrain the architectural language through libraries of predetermined architectural elements. Robert Aish explains:

'There was a direct mapping between what was thought to be an architectural vocabulary of : "walls, windows and doors" and a simplified computational equivalent. Maybe this was all that could be implemented at the time. But the net result, and disastrous at that, was to entrench this highly limited form of architecture by making it "more efficient" and excluding to architecture based on more general geometry or less conventional components and configurations. What is different with recent parametric design tools is that the set of constructs is far more abstract, but at the same time the system is "extensible", so that it is the designer who can make his own vocabulary of components. We have broken the "hard-coded" naive architectural semantics. We are no longer interested in "local efficiency" within a restrictive CAD system, but rather the designer has the opportunity to define his own vocabulary from first principles, by first understanding the underlying geometric and algebraic abstractions.'

A parametric approach to design has already been in use in the aero, automotive, naval and product design industries. In fact, most related software applications are spin-offs from these industries. All of the SmartGeometry members were users or developers of some of the early parametric software for mechanical engineering and naval architecture. Hugh Whitehead and Robert Aish explain their views on concepts of parametric applications in those fields, comparing them to architecture and outlining the group's strategies for developing a new parametric design application as follows:

'Production industries for the engineering of cars, ships and aircraft are geared to minimise tooling costs by creating a range of standard models from mass-produced custom components. On the other hand, construction industries for the architecture of buildings aim to create one-off custom designs, but with an economy based on the use of standardised components. Of course, this is a simplistic historical view. However, it aims to highlight the different approaches of the two industry sectors. Both achieve a variety of products while exploiting standardisation in different ways to achieve efficiency. The advent of digital fabrication techniques has made possible the concept of "mass customisation", which is blurring this distinction and thereby allowing industries to learn from each other and also to borrow technologies. But the core technology for the shift resides in software engineering.

'The success of a piece of software is about the match or mismatch of assumptions between the software designer and the users. We can say that we all learnt from the assumptions made by the software developers of these other parametric systems for other industries. We learnt about what was transferable to architecture and we learnt what additional functionality would be required if the transition of parametric design to architecture was to be successful. There are two important characteristics of parametric design applied to aircraft or ship design that are not present in terrestrial architecture. The first is that concepts and configurations change relatively slowly. Secondly, a single design, with some minor variations, will be used for a production run of ten, hundreds, or possibly thousands of instances. Therefore, there is the time and resources to invest in the proper "genotype" and ensure that this can support the anticipated variations in the phenotypes. Contrast this with buildings where, in the main, each one is unique. There is no time or need to develop a highly adaptive genotype. There is only one instance so there is no need for a genotype that can support variations in the phenotype.

'There are three exceptions to this statement. First, with a building such as a sports stadium, which is distinctly "rule-based", it may be advantageous to develop a strong genotype the characteristics of which can be refined and shared with successive variants. Second, a building such as the Grimshaw Waterloo International Railway Terminal contains "variation" within a single configuration. In this case, establishing a viable genotype for the characteristic "banana" truss was an essential prerequisite for the design. Third, all design can benefit from refinement. We don't just build the first idea. The intellectual processes of externalisation, generalisation and abstraction that are essential in aircraft or ship design to define the genotype can also benefit a one-off building design. However, the important difference with terrestrial architecture is the rapid exploration of alternative configurations. This requirement for the convenient exploration of alternative configurations adds an important requirement to the functionality of parametric design tools. Thus it seemed to be of prime importance to create a system with great flexibility, particularly in the form and content of "collections".

'Buildings are collections of objects. If the design changes, as it will or should do, then these collections of objects have to respond. The content of the collections will change, and the individual members of the collection also have to respond uniquely to changes in their specific context. If we wish to support a flexible approach to design, then this requires that the concept of flexibility and responsiveness is programmed in from the very initial thoughts about the application, and then this concept has to be consistently implemented. But what this also means is that designers who use this software must understand how to control this type of flexibility, how to think abstractly about design with an "algebra of collections". The question is whether the need to understand and be completely conversant with a formal notation is acceptable to architects and designers. Is it either an essential way to add precision to the expression of design intent or an imposition that distracts from an intuitive sense of design? Historically architecture successfully combined different ways of thinking that spanned both the intuitive and the formal. So there is a strong precedence established. Of late, the formal component has been somewhat lacking, again with notable exceptions. Certainly the emerging architectural practices being started by the new generation of graduates emerging from architectural schools have no inhibitions in moving effortlessly between these two approaches and producing impressive results.'

One of the focal points of the group's work in synergising their individual expertise in a unique collaboration spanning the worlds of practice, research and education is the development of the GenerativeComponents software. All of the group's members contribute in different ways to the evolution of the software, and they are in agreement that 'the specification of GenerativeComponents is intentionally open-ended and generic in order to provide an integrated environment for design and development that is not tied to any specific industry or workflow conventions. It aims to support the evolution of ideas by exposing the language and making this accessible to both designer and developer in a consistent manner at all levels of interaction.'

Robert Aish, who is leading the development of GenerativeComponents as Bentley's Director of Research, more specifically explains the key concepts of this next generation of CAD software:

'We can describe GenerativeComponents as an "object oriented, feature based" modelling system and development environment that represents the convergence of design theory with computational theory. The GenerativeComponents technology is based on the following eight key concepts:

1 Implication: the ability to define "long-chain" associativity of geometric constructs, allowing the implications of change to be explored via automatic change propagation
2 Conditional modelling: the ability to encode and exercise alternative implications allowing changes in behaviour or configuration of the geometric construct
3 Extensibility: the ability to turn parametric models into new reusable components, where behaviour of the component is defined by the original model
4 Components: the transition from digital components representing discrete physical entities to devices for cognitive structuring
5 Replication: the ability to operate on sets of digital components, potentially where each set member can uniquely respond to variations in its context
6 Programmatic design: the ability to combine declarative representations in the form of an implication structure and procedural representations

7 Multiple representations: the ability for the user to simultaneously create and operate on different, complementary, linked representations
8 Transactional model of design: representations are an editable, re-executable design history.

'All software is based on the concept of representation, so what is being represented with GenerativeComponents? Superficially, what the user sees on the screen is geometry that might represent some building or other more general design, but this is not the primary representation. At the next level of depth, GenerativeComponents is explicitly modelling the dependency or other more general relationships between geometry and other nongraphic elements such as variables, expressions, conditional statement and scripts. Again, this is not the primary representation. What is effectively being represented are design decisions or, more correctly, a "transactional" model that allows a sequence of alternative decisions to be constructed, exercised and evaluated. This corresponds to the process of design at its most fundamental.

Parametric design systems are introducing a whole new set of concepts, based on design theory, computational theory and object-oriented software engineering that may be quite unfamiliar to practising designers.

Nonetheless, parametric design systems are introducing a whole new set of concepts, based on design theory, computational theory and object-oriented software engineering that may be quite unfamiliar to practising designers. Yet the intention of GenerativeComponents is to apply these concepts in a way that is directly related and beneficial to the process of design.'

Some of these concepts have already been implemented in practice by members of the group in close collaboration with project-specific design teams. With the aim of exploiting advantages of parametric design processes, new ways of enabling and structuring the development of geometrically complex buildings have been established. Hugh Whitehead explains how such a parametric approach to design has become instrumental for the work of Foster and Partners:

'At Foster and Partners the Specialist Modelling Group provides inhouse consultancy to project teams at all stages from concept design to detailed fabrication. Although we provide tools, techniques and workflow, these are developed in the reverse order. Starting with the formulation of the problem, the first step is to propose an appropriate workflow. Within this frame of reference, suitable techniques are tried and tested in different combinations. The results then form the brief for the development of custom tools that are tested by the design team in a continuing dialogue. Custom tool-building ensures that a rationale becomes an integral part of the design concept. This then allows for the generation and control of more complex building geometries.

'In addition to the Smithsonian Institute project [see overleaf], another interesting example is the Swiss Re building that forced us to address the problem of how to design and produce details that are programmed rather than drawn. At each floor, the rules are always the same, but the results are always different. At the same time, even if every plan, section and elevation could have been drawn, this still would not adequately describe the design intent, even for tender purposes let alone construction. The building stands as a classic example of an associative framework providing a context for adaptive parametric components, so that fabrication follows a consistent dialogue between structural and cladding node geometry. The designer is in charge of the rehearsal, but the contractor is responsible for the performance. We are limited in what we can build by what we are able to communicate. Many of the problems we now face are problems of language rather than technology. The experience of Swiss Re established successful procedures for communicating design through a geometry method statement.

'Complex geometries involve very large parameter sets that are impossible to control by direct manipulation. With buildings like the Beijing airport, which has a double-curved roof that is 3 kilometres long, the approach was to develop control mechanisms that can be driven by law curves. Law curves control "rate of change" and can be geometric as graphs or algebraic as functions. By representing higher derivatives as curves, or even surfaces, complex behaviour can be achieved with simple manipulation.'

Such a parametric and editable approach to design offers a high degree of geometric control combined with the ability to rapidly generate variations. All of the group's members agree that parametric models therefore seem to be particularly versatile in providing the relevant information for digital performance tests. However, the requirements for different analysis methods need to be considered. Whitehead continues:

'Digital performance tests are carried out in collaboration with external consultants. This involves many different software applications and operating systems, but more importantly each requires a different simplified representation of the model as the input to their analysis routines. Structural analysis requires centre lines, thermal analysis requires volumes, acoustic analysis requires simple planes, and daylight analysis requires meshes. The more complex and detailed the model, the more difficult it is to decompose to an appropriate level of simplification. Because of the cost of simplifying or rebuilding models, consultants prefer to engineer a design only when the configuration has become stable. However, when the model is generative, it becomes easier to produce multiple representations, which remain associative to the conceptual framework. This ability allows one to track comparative options and to perform more iteration of the analysis cycles. Consequently, the main impact of such an approach on the practice of architecture is on the decision-making process. Previously the designer had to freeze the early strategic decisions in order to progress to increasing levels of detail. This involved cyclic explorations, but the early decisions can only be challenged if there are both time and resources to rework the downstream details. In a parametric approach, the ability to populate an associative framework with adaptive components allows us to defer the decision-making process until we are ready to evaluate the results.'

Parametric modelling has been understood as instrumental for its ability in improving workflow, its rapid adaptability to changing input and its delivery of precise geometric data for digital fabrication and performance analysis. But while accelerating and extending established design processes, the skills and techniques developed by the SmartGeometry Group do also inherently challenge the way we think about the design of buildings. One may argue that novel aspects in architecture emerge when deeply entrenched typologies, conventions and preconceptions of the organisation and materialisation of the built environment are challenged and rethought by the design team. The SmartGeometry Group envisions their approach to design to become instrumental for such processes of rethinking architecture. Hugh Whitehead explains:

'As of yet, designers use sketches and models to externalise a thought process, in order to provide both focus and stimulus for the development of shared ideas. The use of generative techniques that are editable promotes a higher level of awareness. It encourages all preconceptions to be challenged because they must first be formulated in language.'

Robert Aish concludes by highlighting the group's awareness of the importance of developing a culture of use of generative techniques in parallel to the digital tools themselves:

'In general, there is a shift in many human activities from "doing" to "controlling", involving the development of tools and a "culture of use" of these tools. Design as a discipline emerges from the craft process as a way of abstracting and evaluating alternative possible configurations, usage scenarios and materialisations without actually physically making and testing each possible alternative. Design involves many analogues of the finished artefact that, with varying fidelity, simulate or indicate the anticipated behaviour of the yet to be built result. These analogues, the design medium, introduce representational and manipulation techniques that may be interesting or attractive in their own right, and these may start to influence the resulting physical outcomes. Seen from this perspective, the development of computational design tools, including parametric tools, may not be too different to development of preceding design tools or to the development of tools in general.

'What we need to focus on is the relationship between the development of these tools and the corresponding development of the skills and the culture of use.'

Robert Aish, Bentley Systems, GenerativeComponents Parametric Design Software Development

Design involves both exploration and the resolution of ambiguity. Therefore, it is not sufficient that computational design tools can model a static representation of a design. What is important is that the design tools are able to capture both the underlying design rules from which a range of potential solutions can be explored, and facilitate how this 'solution space' can be refined into a suitable candidate for construction. The question is, how can these design rules be represented and how can this exploration and refinement process be supported? By way of illustration, let us consider the issues involved when a roof, initially based on a doubly curved freeform surface, is required to be constructed from planar components. Here, the designer might want to explore simultaneously two interrelated aspects of the design: alternative surface configurations and alternative penalisation strategies.

To model not just one solution to this problem, but the design rules that can be used to explore alternative solutions, requires a complex 'graph' of 'associative geometry'. The system of geometric relationships illustrated here is quite complex to understand, even when presented with the finished model. It is necessary to imagine how more complex it was to originate the model. Our contention as software developers is that a 3-D geometric representation, while essential, would be insufficient to describe the complex geometric associativities required to present the underlying design rules. So in addition to the standard geometry model (Figure 1) we include a symbolic model (Figure 2) that externalises and presents these relationships in an explicit graphical form. Also represented is a law curve 'controller' (Figure 3) that provides a geometric input at one stage removed from the geometric models and the flat pattern layout of the panels (Figure 4) ready for laser cutting. (In this context, the law curve is controlling the elevation profile of the roof surface, independently of the plan 'S' configuration of the 'spine' curve.)

What variations does this model allow us to explore? a) the poles of the spine curve can be moved in Cartesian space; b) the position of the planes on the spine curve can be moved in 1-D parametric space (along the spine curve); c) the poles of the cross-sectional curves can be moved in the 2-D planar space; d) the number and spacing of the points on the surface can be defined within the surface's 2-D parameter space; e) various alternative 'lacing' options are available to use the points on the surface to populate either planar or nonplanar quadrilateral or triangular panels; and f) the order of the spine curves and cross-sectional curves can be varied. Having defined this process, the designer can then explore variations within the solution space, not in some rigid parametric way, but by using an intuitive process of 'direct manipulation' and 'hand–eye coordination'.

Here, the designer can graphically select and manipulate one of the control points of the law curve model and observe: a) the law curve update; b) the cross-section curves update; c) the surface update; d) the points on the surface update; e) the quadrilateral panels on the surface update; and f) the planar unfolded fabrication model update. The whole process is being intuitively controlled in dynamics with the designer completely in control of the 'form making' process and its materialisation. While these variations are reasonably complex, it should be stressed that they are only the variations that can be explored within this particular logical and geometric configuration. The designer can also change the configuration (by editing the relationships in the symbolic model), which then opens up alternative ranges of variations to be explored.

To arrive at this level of expression and control required that the designer had to be skilled in the logic of design, in order to define and refine the complex system of geometric, algebraic and logical relationships that is the essential foundation of this process. Ultimately, it is this combination of intuition and logic, of ideas and skills, that is of interest.

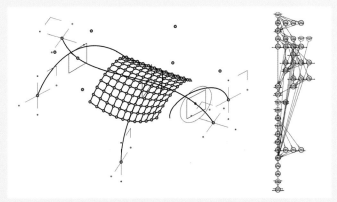

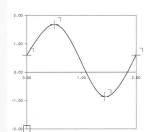
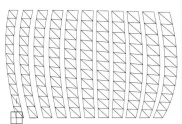

Figure 1 (left): Geometry model. Figure 2 (right): Symbolic model of the same parametric geometry of a double-curved surface.

Figure 3 (left): Law curve 'controller' of parametric surface model. Figure 4 (right): Flat pattern layout of its faces.

Hugh Whitehead, Brady Peters and Francis Aish, SMG **Foster and Partners, Specialist Modelling Group, Smithsonian Institute Courtyard Enclosure, Washington** DC**, 2004**

In 2004, Foster and Partners won an invited international architecture competition to design a new courtyard enclosure for the Smithsonian Institute's Patent Office building in Washington DC. Early in the project, the Specialist Modelling Group was brought in to advise the project team on modelling techniques, to develop new digital tools, and help solve the complex geometric issues involved. Norman Foster's early sketch shows a diagonal grid of structural elements gently flowing over the central courtyard. The undulating roof structure is supported by eight columns arranged in three domes, the central peak being the highest and having the greatest span.

Instead of simply translating a sketch, capturing design intent involves the development of a digital schematic that can be easily used by the designers to control and manipulate the complex geometry. Design constraints are encoded within a system of associated geometries. Three surfaces, column markers and a computer script control the entire roof geometry. Constraints such as edge beam location, dome heights and drainage locations are informed by the design surface, which is created from a series of simple control lines. The parameterisation of the grid surface sets out the plan locations of the design nodes, while the height location is given by the design surface. The relationship between these surfaces and a third surface controls the beam twist. The set-out geometry performs as a mechanism to control the parameters of a generative script.

Using the set-out geometry and a set of parameter values, a computer script creates a variety of detailed roof components. The script adapts each component to its local condition and, through a performance evaluation, the components respond to their environment. The use of scripting as a design approach provided many benefits:

1 The simultaneous generation of multiple representations within a single model; a centre-line model for structural analysis; a triangulated flat-panel model for acoustic analysis; a simplified model for hidden line visualisations; lighting node position models; node and beam set-out drawings and spreadsheets; unfolded beams for the digital fabrication of scale models; and a complete model of all roof elements for the creation of drawings by the project team.
2 The independent development of roof configuration and individual component strategies. The roof geometry was free to change without affecting the logic of the beam section or panelisation system. Within the script, different modules of code could be inserted, removed or edited to create new roof options. Using this approach, the long-chain dependencies of a fully associative system did not exist, and modification was simpler and regeneration much faster. When changes were made to the script or to the set-out geometry, a new digital model could be generated rapidly. A dynamically parametric model was not necessary.
3 A computer-generated model gave very precise control over the values and relationships within the roof system. It produced consistent and repeatable results where the design history was saved as a copy of the generating script and the set-out geometry used.

The design evolution involved the use of many different media and techniques and an intense dialogue between a large team and many consultants. The script became a synthesis of all the design ideas and was constantly modified and adapted during the design process. Scripting was used as a sketching tool to test new ideas. This explorative approach required knowledge of both programming and architectural design combined with interpretative skills on many levels. It proved a fast and flexible approach. The final version of this generating code was 5000 lines in length and had 57 parameters – some numeric values and others switch-controlling options. Using only the set-out geometry as input, the script generated approximately 120,000 elements in about 15 seconds; 415 models were generated over six months.

It is possible to generate thousands of different options by using scripting. It therefore becomes increasingly important to not only understand the system constraints, but to have a clear strategy for evaluating the generated options. The design was evaluated by many methods: structural, environmental, acoustic and aesthetic. While there was no attempt to automate the feedback process, it did prove beneficial to work closely with consultants to better understand their data-input needs for their analyses. By building the production of this information into the script, the generation/analysis cycle could be shortened. Working closely with the structural engineers, Buro Happold, reduced the time taken for the generation/analysis loop. As well as creating traditional visualisations and animations, a new technique was employed in which an image set was automatically generated and reviewed for a matrix of options. In parallel, the physical production of digitally fabricated scale models and the production of 1:1 mock-ups was critical to the decision-making process.

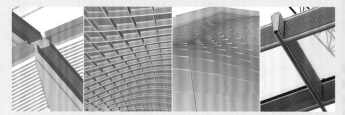

Digital detail of roof beam connection and gutter arrangement (left) of the roof structure (centre left); flat panel solution for glazing panels arrayed on double-curved roof surface (centre right); and related full-scale mock-up of roof beams and glazing built at the Gartner HQ in Gundelfingen, Germany (right).

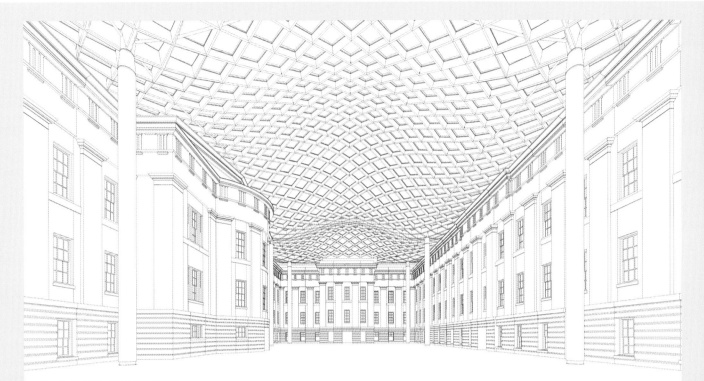

Courtyard enclosure interior study.

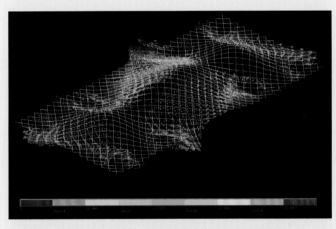

Above: Structural analysis of rotational deflections under self-weight.
Below: Analysis of average daily insulation on roof panels without shading device (top) and with shading device (bottom).

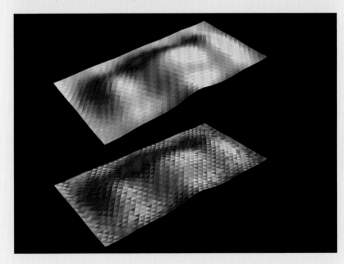

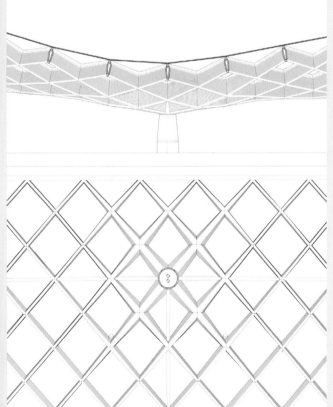

Elevation of column and section through roof beams (top) and reflected plan of column and roof beam connection (bottom).

Lars Hesselgren and Stylianos Dritsas, KPF London,
Bishopsgate Tower, City of London, 2005

The Bishopsgate Tower project utilises only simple geometry – lines and tangent arcs – in order to facilitate manufacture. The footprint polygon is carefully calibrated to fit the site. The setting out progresses from the root point of the building, and the primary geometry is a set of tapered planes chamfered with sheared cones. The taper on each plane provides the only control mechanism within the geometric system to control the taper of the sheared cones. The helical crown is a solution to the visual problem posed by the viewing of the building from multiple points.

The parametric modelling allowed easy tuning of the exact height of the crown. To achieve natural control of the helical curve in space, a 'normalised graph' was built. The visual verification of the crown results in the curve having a slight 'S' shape. The essential rule for the structural system is that it is offset from the design skin. Each column has its centre-line on a vector that is parallel to the setting-out geometry, with the result that all columns are straight and no column is vertical. The mullions are on a simple module set out linearly from the point of origin and, since the building tapers, the modules are offset, introducing shear in the facade.

To achieve natural ventilation there is an outer glass skin made of flat, planar glass panels of identical size. The panels are tipped in space to create overlaps both in plan and on section, which act as ventilation spaces. The system for establishing correct overlap involved the development of a programmed extension to the parametric system. The selected methodology respects the attitude of a particular panel with respect to its neighbours. The canopy is tangential to the main design surface

The springing height is horizontal and supports the unique arc, which is tangential at the plane of every planning module vector. Each arc is divided into a harmonic series based on the length of the arc. Each set of points is connected longitudinally, forming the centre-lines of the canopy 'hoops', which are doubly curved in space.

for aesthetic and aerodynamic reasons. The differing requirements along the canopy length, ranging from near vertical sections to 'peaked hat' lift-up sections for protecting and signalling entrances, is solved by an edge curve driven by two law curves. The springing height is horizontal and supports the unique arc, which is tangential at the plane of every planning module vector. Each arc is divided into a harmonic series based on the length of the arc. Each set of points is connected longitudinally forming the centre-lines of the canopy 'hoops', which are doubly curved in space.

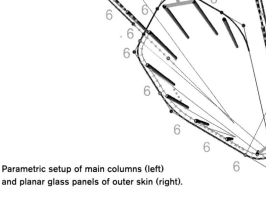

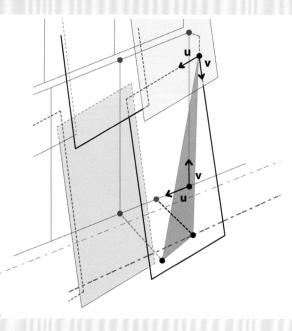

Parametric setup of main columns (left)
and planar glass panels of outer skin (right).

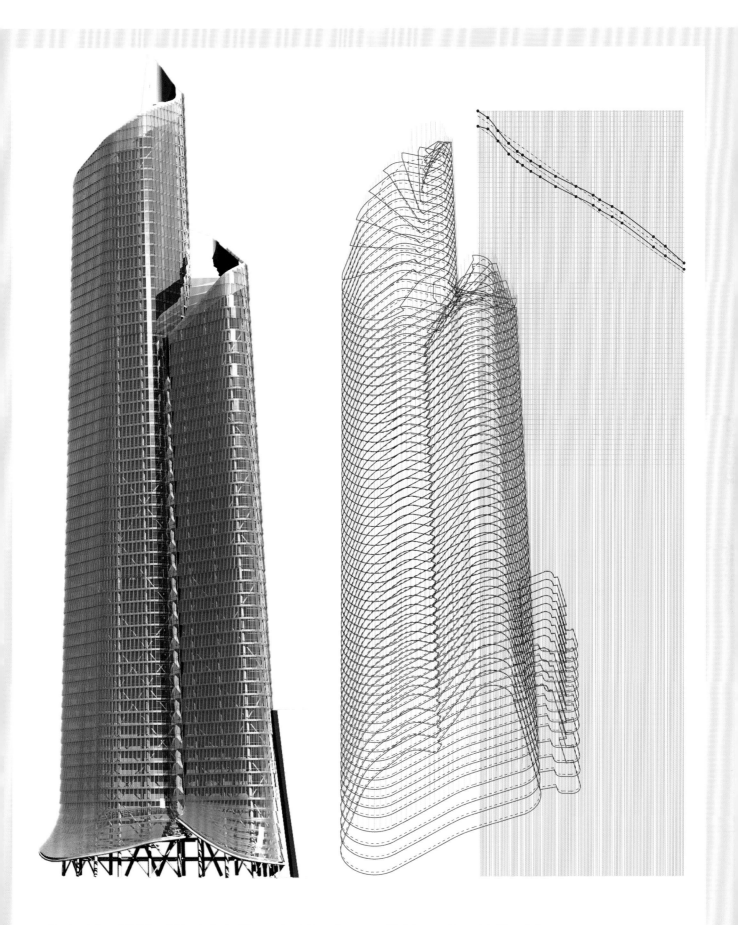

Rendered view of digital model (rendering by Cityscape/model by KPF).

Digital parametric model with control curves.

Parametric model of the folded generative component (bottom),
and proliferation of component in one design solution (top).

Digital model of one design solution for a folded-plate roof structure.

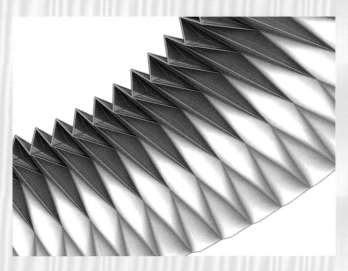

surface-active structures. Compression and tensile forces are measured as continuous force-flows across the whole length of the structure. These force-flows may differ to quite an extent depending on the way local or regional scale components are assembled.

Differentiation of the regularity of the structure must be carefully studied for its structural, as well as its geometric, implications. A physical origami-like structure maintains its triangular surface-area dimensions when translational and/or rotational operations are applied. Assuming the global geometry of the roof structure was nonuniform in nature, and given that the design required the differentiation of the folded-plate geometry according to structural load, the aim was to construct a digital parametric model that would mimic the behaviour of the physical paper model and could be informed, beyond the geometrical logic of the system, by structural performance.

This folded-plate structure was modelled in Bentley's GenerativeComponents software, creating an environment that supported the adaptive exploration of the design solution. The local-scale component was comprised of six plates connected to one common vertex; all surface areas of the elements were maintained constant when translational and rotational operations were applied. The global-scale model consisted of approximately 400 plates and has, on the other hand, confirmed the doubt that when constrained to the global geometry restrictions posed by the two nonconcentric arcs, the plate surface dimensions will gradually change by a given increment across the longitudinal section of the roof. ⌀

Lars Hesselgren and Neri Oxman, KPF London, Folded-Plate Roof research project, 2005

This project is a research-oriented work in progress. It was designed as a differentiated lightweight folded-plate structure that can be suspended between two masses of a building. The base geometrical plan layout is comprised of two nonconcentric arcs. The total arc length is approximately 100 metres (330 feet), and the span dimensions range from 7 to 16 metres (23 to 52 feet). In such classes of surface-active structures, the structural surfaces can be composed to form mechanisms that redirect forces. Therefore, structural continuity of the elements in two axes (surface resistance against compressive, tensile and shear stresses) is the first prerequisite and first distinction of

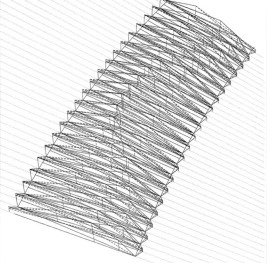

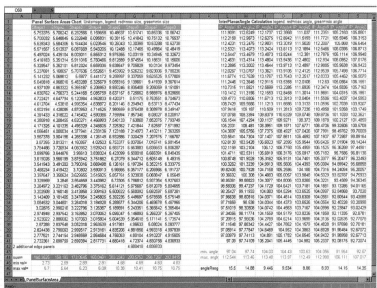

Parametric model of folded-plate roof project with spreadsheet of digitally derived geometric data.

Advanced Simulation in Design

Simulations are essential for designing complex material systems, and for analysing their behaviour over extended periods of time. As **Michael Weinstock** and **Nikolaos Stathopoulos** explain, working with simulations requires the development of a mathematical model of physical processes, and generative computational design can now inexpensively incorporate the advanced physics of nonlinear behaviour to explore the dynamic changes that structures and materials undergo in response to changing conditions.

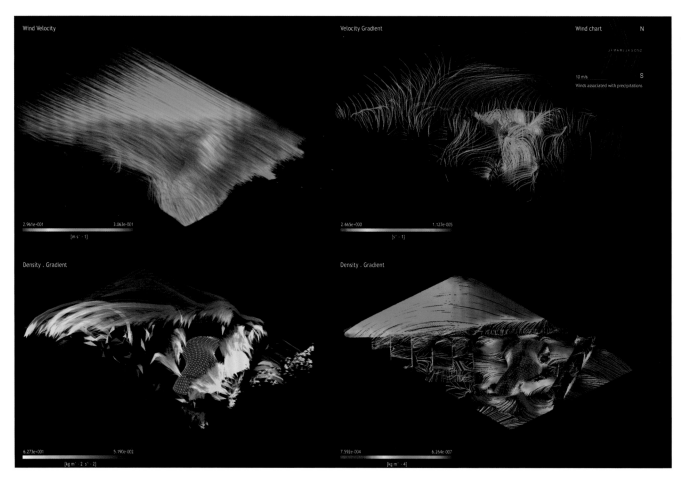

Visualisation of the main wind-flow parameters around proposed building on a site in Chile. The focus of the wind-flow simulation is on wind patterns at the scale of the site and the effect of the natural and built topography on the wind-flow patterns. Velocity streamlines in different directions and pressure gradients are shown, with colour coding that represents the value or intensity of the parameters. Work from the dissertation of Juan Subercaseaux, Emergent Technologies and Design Masters programme, AA Graduate School of Architecture, 2005, with Nikolaos Stathopoulos as simulation and visualisation consultant.

Much of the physical environment can be simulated in the computer: a simple 'Google' search will show a collection of sites on the web that have interactive simulations of physics principles, including light, optics, springs and masses, pendulums and waves, harmonics, mechanics and momentum, and even nuclear physics. In such simulations, the parameters of objects can be modified and the resultant change in behaviour observed.

Most architectural design software now includes sunlight modelling for any location in the world, and an increasing range of plug-ins or scripts can simulate the behaviour of chains and springs under gravity. More sophisticated simulations, such as the stress response of structures under imposed loads, or the flow of air and heat through spaces and in materials, are standard modules in engineering software.

Engineering Simulations

The studio of the Emergent Technologies and Design (Emtech) Masters programme at the AA Graduate School of Architecture uses Ansys software for the analysis of natural structural systems, and for the simulations shown here. For simulation, Ansys Multiphysics is the most comprehensive software – a coupled physics 'engine' that enables us to construct and run simulations for structural, thermal, fluid dynamics, acoustic and electromagnetic analysis. The studio also uses the new desktop simulation environment Ansys Workbench to simulate the wind-flow patterns and pressures developing on a building envelope of a given global geometry at different times during the year, for a site in Chile. Design student Juan Subercaseaux has used simulations as part of the design development for an adaptive facade system that utilises components that locally alter the permeability of, and are distributed across, the building envelope. The careful analysis of wind-flow patterns and pressures on the building envelope produced by the simulation is used to develop a strategy for controlling the localised facade components in a coordinated way, so that the wind characteristics of the site are used for natural ventilation and passive environmental modulation.

Setting up the simulation required two sets of data: gathering and analysing meteorological information for the site and the predominant wind speeds and their directionality, and producing 3-D models of the building and the surrounding topography, natural and built, within a region of approximately half a kilometre.

Using simulation techniques in emergent technologies and design is not limited to using engineering software, but also includes the use of animation software familiar to a wider design community (Maya), and the scripting capabilities and solvers on offer for developing custom simulation tools. Giorgos Kailis, a former Emergent Technologies and Design student with a background in engineering, studied the physics and self-organisation characteristics of tensioned membranes and used MEL scripting to reproduce a stress-relaxation simulation in the Maya Dynamics Environment. Maya was extended to make it a tool capable of simulating the process of a membrane settling to a minimum energy shape when fixed in a number of points in space. Simulating this process for membranes with different starting cutting patterns proved a valuable tool during the manufacturing of a series of physical prototypes of the membrane-tensegrity structural system.

Simulation is used increasingly in practice by consultants from various disciplines and for the purpose of evaluating different performance aspects of a design. The acoustics simulation conducted by ArupAcoustics for the Greater London Assembly (GLA) building is a very good example of advanced simulation used for evaluating the quality – in this case acoustic – of a space, in a way that would not have been possible via other means. The unusual geometry of the main theatre of the building makes it very difficult to predict the acoustics of the space by the conventional method of comparisons from observations and data of existing buildings. The many well-established rules of thumb for the acoustic design of spaces cannot be applied to such complex geometries. Simulation allowed the evaluation of the acoustic performance and properties of the space, and identified problematic surfaces and areas early in the design process, so that subsequent modifications to the design improved the performance of the space, and were subsequently incorporated into the design of the building.

It is sometimes said that modelling the nonlinear behaviour of the cyclic loads on structural components and soil during an earthquake with enough confidence to predict actual behaviour is an intractable problem. Using Ansys,

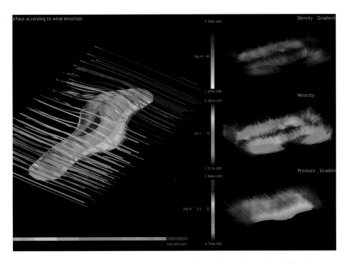

Study of velocity streamlines and pressure gradients focusing on local effects on the building envelope. Work from the dissertation of Juan Subercaseaux, Emergent Technologies and Design Masters programme, AA Graduate School of Architecture, 2005, with Nikolaos Stathopoulos as simulation and visualisation consultant.

ArupAcoustics, Greater London Assembly,
London, 2002
Simulation and visualisation of acoustic waves
propagation, refraction and attenuation in the
assembly chamber. The simulation is based on
the original AutoCAD drawings of the architect
and produces a visualisation of the acoustical
characteristics of the space.

simulation of the performance of structural systems during an earthquake is based on historic earthquake data in order to develop synthetic earthquake time histories. Simulating the cyclic loads is not the real difficulty, as there is enough data from observed events. It is in the interactions of components in the structure that the difficulty lies: for example, when a small failure causes the global redistribution of stress. These kinds of simulations need to be based on the observed behaviour of materials and components, and verified using data from physical experiments. New designs for structures in earthquake-sensitive areas can be better developed if these simulations are used in the generation of designs, rather than for the optimisation of earthquake proofing of 'finished' designs.

Open System for Earthquake Engineering Simulation (OpenSees) is an advanced simulation software that is useful for the analysis of hypothetical and representative scenarios for structural behaviour, and for soil and foundation behaviour. OpenSees is open source, freely available from Berkeley University as application program interface (API) that is fully documented and offers examples and data, solution methods, equation solving, databases and visualisation.

Engineering simulations in fields other than architecture are well developed, and suggest new directions for research within architecture and engineering. In medicine, for example, the Centre for Biomaterials and Tissue at Sheffield University is developing simulations for biological materials. As in the Emtech research regarding the behaviour of plant systems, 3-D models are subjected to stresses, and the response then studied. These simulations are revealing the movements of human tissues under stress, and of the fluids within the tissues. Simulations that accurately simulate the behaviour of living human tissue are extremely valuable for medicine in general, and in particular for the design of prostheses.

Simulations developed from fluid dynamics are useful for modelling the flow of blood through the heart, indicating flow situations of high shear that may damage blood corpuscles. Damaged corpuscles tend to form clots, which are always dangerous, but especially so for patients with implants such as artificial valves and stents. Engineering simulations are used in the design and development of such implants. Simulation of the dynamic behaviour of the lungs,

a joint research of Sheffield University and the University of Mainz in Germany, is being developed for the direct delivery of medicines, and promising an extremely direct diffusion through the alveolus into the patient's bloodstream. The fluid dynamics of the air-filled spaces of the lungs is nonlinear, and no doubt more complex than the environmental simulations currently used in architectural engineering. The value of this kind of simulation for the generation of responsive architectural 'skins' and for adaptive intelligent environmental systems for buildings is evident.

Urban Simulations

SimCity is an interesting game, a simulation in which the game engine simulates the complex growth of cities, with the player able to alter many parameters and see the effects of the interaction between taxes, zoning, infrastructure, pollution, topography and so on. It is iterative and interactive and, within the limits of the gaming industry, is a remarkable growth simulation. Its limitation is that the model of urban development cannot be modified, so that neither development

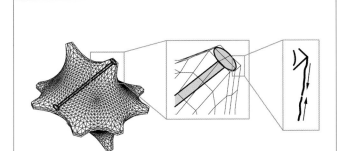

Geometry of the membrane-tensegrity structure produced by the simulation process and detail of the forces' transfer between the tensioned membrane and the compression rods when the system has reached equilibrium. Work from the dissertation of Giorgos Kailis, Emergent Technologies and Design Masters programme, 2003.

Dynamic relaxation process simulated in Maya. Different stages of the relaxation process lead to a final minimum energy surface geometry and an equilibrium state for the overall structure.

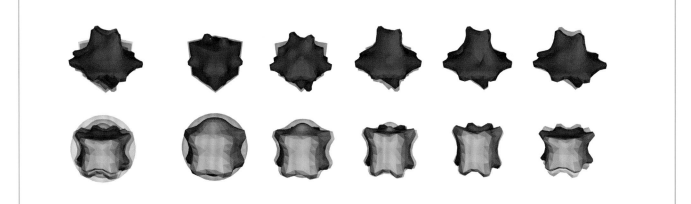

Digital stress-driven form evolution of membrane tensegrity structures.

Cities are complex systems. The flow of vehicles and people within a city represents the emergent behaviour of such a system, produced by the large numbers of decisions of the individuals, and their interaction with each other and with the transport infrastructure of the city. Complex systems are, by definition, nonlinear and sensitive to initial conditions, so that small changes in such conditions may produce turbulent behaviour at the global scale.

of multi-use vertical programming of buildings, urban blocks and zones, nor the integration of variable-flow multiphase transport interchanges with 'air rights' are possible. If it was possible to alter the model the simulation 'engine' uses, SimCity would be a useful tool for evaluating hypothetical urban developments and urban flow that would be impossible to observe in the physical world.

Cities are complex systems. The flow of vehicles and people within a city represents the emergent behaviour of such a system, produced by the large numbers of decisions of the individuals, and their interaction with each other and with the transport infrastructure of the city. Complex systems are, by definition, nonlinear and sensitive to initial conditions, so that small changes in such conditions may produce turbulent behaviour at the global scale. There are two strategies for the task of modelling a complex system. The simplest and fastest is to abstract mathematical descriptions from the observed behaviour of an existing system, and to model the overall distributions of identifiable patterns and parameters. For example, traffic simulations are often constructed from known patterns of behaviour in fluid dynamics, and combined with parameters for velocity and density in the traffic network. Simulations constructed in this way are economic with regard to the computational time and resources required, they run quickly and reliably produce behaviours that are generally indicative.

An alternative bottom-up approach starts from the recognition that a complex system is a very large number of small and simple components, each of which is semi-autonomous but interacts with its neighbours. The behaviour of the global system emerges from the interactions and local behaviours of the individual components or agents. It is widely noted in many sciences that this approach produces the degree of complexity observed in the physical world. Agent-based software builds detailed and complex behaviours for individual entities from simple rules, and the ability to modify the behaviour is critically important. Behaviour of people in the city is not a reliable constant, tending to change with weather, time and place. Multi-agent-based software is inherently distributed, and well suited to deployment on a network, and it is sometimes suggested that this type of simulation, incorporating local information and control, combined with the interaction of individuals, is a new software paradigm for simulations, despite the fact that it is exceptionally demanding on computational resources. An ideal system would incorporate both approaches, and would be very useful in the design studio for complex urban design.

Manufacturing, Construction and Material Simulations

In aerospace, maritime and automotive engineering, physical behaviour, including wear and fatigue throughout the life of the vehicle, is simulated during the design phase. In many industries, manufacturing processes are also simulated digitally in the design studio. The actual tool paths of a computer numerically controlled (CNC) router can be run digitally prior to the physical production run, and this is now part of all computer-controlled manufacturing processes. Simulation of the machine processes of CNC, rapid prototyping and laser cutting is normally part of the procedure of preparing designs for fabrication, and now extends to the casting, milling, extrusion and bending machines by which many architectural components are now produced. Simulations allow the development and refinement of designs prior to the construction of physical models and prototypes. The simulation of prototyping, sometimes known as 'virtual prototyping', usually requires multiple iterative dynamic simulations prior to the production of a physical rapid prototype.

Simulations of manufacturing processes such as cutting, welding and heat treatments are used to predict the material properties of manufactured components. This is especially important as some thermomechanical processes tend to distort the form of a component or modify its material properties. There are a number of well-developed simulation methodologies within 'virtual manufacturing'. However, even though simulations are frequently in use, these are usually simulations of singular processes, rather than the complete sequence of manufacturing processes that most artefacts will pass through, from raw material to installed component. A sequence of analyses of manufacturing processes requires a system for the exchange of information between different softwares, as most engineering software will solve problems

As architects become more accustomed to working directly with construction manufacturers at the inception of a design, the potential benefits of integrating manufacturing processes into the design generation will become more evident and more widely adopted.

within a single domain. Standardised formats such as IGES and STEP are useful, but the commercial objectives of the software developer often mean that we have to develop translation protocols for data sharing or even redefine boundary conditions and redraw geometrical models. As architects become more accustomed to working directly with construction manufacturers at the inception of a design, the potential benefits of integrating manufacturing processes into the design generation will become more evident and more widely adopted.

The development of new or variant material composites is another area where simulations are enabling rapid innovation and the bypassing of the conventional method of producing small batches of physical samples and subjecting them to tests to determine the properties. The process of testing, modifying the material and producing new samples is usually a long series of repetitive physical experiments and manufacturing processes that continues until a suitable compromise between manufacturing constraints and acceptable performance is reached, and full-scale production can begin. Digital simulations can explore, in a mathematical model, variations of fibre densities, incorporating different kinds of plies in differing orientations in an unlimited number of material formulations. This is known as 'virtual testing' and replaces most, but not all, physical testing, which can be reserved for the final prototypes.

Virtual testing of composites uses a mathematical model to predict the behaviour of the composite under stress, and to predict the changes to the material as stress and subsequent damage increase. The material can be digitally modelled in a specific configuration, such as a membrane, a surface or strut, and subjected to stress parameters that closely resemble the actual stresses the material will be subjected to in use in the physical world. It is possible to do this in most sophisticated finite element packages, but there are also specialised interactive softwares developed for the simulation of the behaviour of composites with the ability to change input parameters, see directly and analyse the effects of changes to the material composition.

Virtual testing is of great value for the design and construction of complex geometry forms and concrete castings. The material properties of concrete develop over time and in situ, and testing usually involves a 28-day wait to assess that the material will reach the required performance. Simulations are used to predict the behaviour and properties of a large range of different 'mixes' and can do so for newly mixed and poured, as well as hardened, concrete. The analysis of concrete flow into formwork is particularly important for the nonstandard forms of contemporary constructions for which no prior data exists. The conventional test, the 'slump test', is a physical experiment that produces limited measurements of the yield stress of concrete flow in known situations.

Concrete flow can only be fully modelled when the viscosity is also known, and such simulations that include changeable parameters can be used to explore the potential means of constructing complex architectural forms. The effect of fibres or aggregates on flow is modelled using a variant of particle dynamics (dissipative particle dynamics) that is rather similar to techniques used for modelling the movement of molecules, but with bigger 'molecules' or aggregate particles. As concrete is a composite, made of materials that vary in size and properties, flow behaviour is nonlinear, and this suggests that the best strategy will be a combination of simulation and physical experiments.

Conclusion

Working with simulations requires the development of a logical mathematical description of the performance of a system or process, which corresponds to certain specific parameters of its physical behaviour. In the sciences, 'model' means more than the geometrical description of an object that we commonly use this term for. A model is an abstraction of a process, and can be refined as understanding of a process develops, so that complex problems can be accurately modelled. Simulations are essential for designing complex material systems, and for analysing their behaviour over extended periods of time.

Simulations, once strictly within the domain of engineering practice, can and should be used as part of the generative design processes in architectural studios. The advanced physics of nonlinear behaviour, and the dynamic changes that structures and materials undergo in response to changing conditions, are all readily and inexpensively available to be incorporated into the architectural design process. Where the design ambition is to develop 'responsive' architectures, buildings or artefacts that have the capacity to make controlled changes to themselves in order to adapt to dynamic loading conditions and environmental changes, advanced simulations are essential. ∆

Differentiation and Performance: Multi-Performance Architectures and Modulated Environments

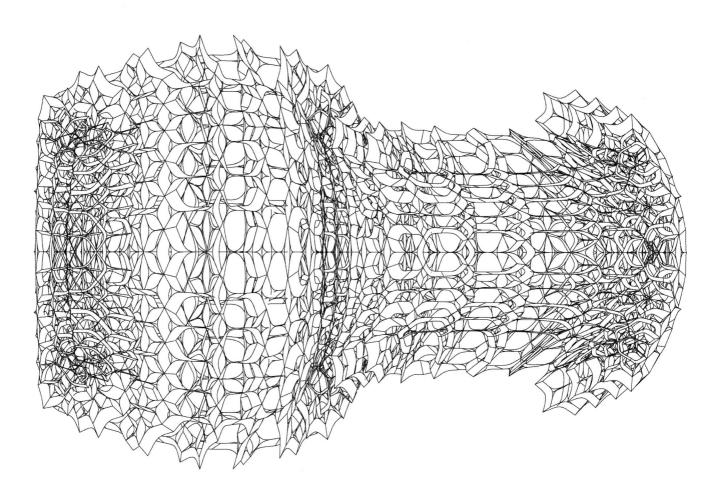

**Daniel Coll I Capdevila, Strip Morphologies, AA Diploma Unit 4
design study for environmentally differentiated healing
environments, London, 2004–05**
View of a parametrically defined strip system differentiated in
response to structural, luminous and sonic performance requirements.

The architectural tradition of the West is fundamentally characterised by substantial structures and building typologies that link tectonics with function and representation.
It has been focusing on the relation between the material constituents that frame space and its direct relation to programme on the one hand, and to social formations on the other. Interior environments are largely homogenised, a preference inherited from Modernist open-plan arrangements and facilitated by vast paraphernalia of electrical and mechanical equipment. Here, **Michael Hensel** and **Achim Menges** argue for an ecological understanding of architecture that promotes the differentiation of environmental conditions through a morphological intelligence, which promises not only a new spatial paradigm for architectural design, but also a far more sustainable one that links the performance capacity of material systems with environmental modulation and the resulting provisions and opportunities for inhabitation.

In his seminal work, *The Architecture of the Well-Tempered Environment,*[1] Reyner Banham describes two traditions of architecture: one with substantial structures and one without. 'Societies who do not build substantial structures inhabit a space whose external boundaries are vague, adjustable and rarely regular,'[2] wrote Banham, referring to the example of a camp fire that provides a gradient of temperature and light that is at the same time dynamically affected by other extrinsic influences, such as airflow and other environmental conditions. These dynamically differentiated spaces provide for the individual preferences of inhabitants. Differentiation is thus expressed in gradient threshold conditions rather than by a hard division between inside and outside, warm and cold, and so on, which Banham posits 'might prove to be of fundamental relevance for power-operated environments'[3] by suggesting a more sustainable approach to architecture.

This article introduces a take on architectural design that incorporates Banham's varied and temporal spatiality into substantial yet equally varied structures, by shifting away from the homogenous and largely monofunctional material systems that make up the built environment today, and towards heterogeneous and multi-performance systems. The aim is to show how these systems can modulate and, in turn, be modulated by environmental conditions, and to suggest alternative spatial strategies based on gradient threshold conditions.

Modernist discourse postulated universal space as the key paradigm for democratic space. The open plan, ideally extended to an infinite homogenous grid, for example, was intended to deliver equal opportunity for inhabitation, while the ribbon window and glass curtain-wall facade was meant to replace privileged framed views. The preference for universal space brought with it the modularisation of building elements and systems, as well as a homogenisation of entire climates. In order to achieve universal space and intended uniformity, each building element or system was required to perform one principal function (such as primary structure, secondary structure, sun shading, rain cover or climate envelope) and was thus optimised towards that particular singular function. This single-objective approach to optimisation is based on an understanding of efficiency that entails the minimum use of material and energy to fulfil one single task.

Single-objective optimisation gave rise to the notion of lightweight structures with minimum use of material to achieve projected structural capacity and performance. With a desired decrease in the use of material came questions of liability that led to an added percentage of performance capacity to guarantee functionality and safety. Thus redundancy was, and still is, largely understood as an unfortunate necessity. A critical view yields the question of whether an alternative understanding of optimisation, efficiency and redundancy in relation to multi-performance material systems can facilitate a very different take on spatial organisation and environmental modulation.

Architectural discourse in the last decades has largely moved away from universal space and declared a preference for heterogeneous architectures. This preference is evident in two distinct strategies. The first entails a two-step approach to varied space, commencing from generic shells that are subsequently tailored to the needs of their eventual inhabitants. The second strategy is the design of exotically shaped buildings that are, from the outset, varied in expression and spatiality. The first strategy embraces modularised building systems, while the second strategy operates on the differentiation of established building elements (for example, individually articulated frames and tile elements). Both strategies concur, however, in embracing standardised requirements for interior environments, such as statistically determined homogenous interior climates for public or office buildings, as well as the limited range of building systems.

The latter is evident in recently developed parametric software that is bound to established engineering and

Unfortunately, environmental design and engineering remains a question of post-design optimisation rather than informing the design process from a very early stage. Moreover, a homogenised interior environment simply cannot satisfy the multiple and contrasting needs of its inhabitants.

OCEAN NORTH, Jyväskylä Music and Art Centre, Phase 02 and 03 design study, London, 2004–05
Perspective view of the interstitial space between and below the volumes of the music hall and rehearsal rooms along the main public circulation trajectory.

manufacturing protocols relative to material and machining technologies. Herein lies the problem. While plan organisation, form of the envelope, or the fittings and finishes might have become more varied, material and building systems are not being critically reviewed with respect to established types and their monofunctionality, as well as building-type-dependent interior climate requirements and uniform condition zoning. Architecture has thus largely remained 'neufertised'.

The homogenisation of interior environments had its first significant peak with the advent of the office landscape approach of the late 1950s through the work of the Quickborner Team für Planung und Organisation, a German management consulting group that proposed vast open-plan arrangements in which the anticipated workflow is manifested in the furnishing of working clusters arranged according to workflow.[4] Applying a large number of rules to the furnished organisation of office space, circulation and workflow, it was argued that a homogenous interior environment would imply the least visual, aural and tactile distraction that needed to be removed. Subsequently, this form of spatial-environmental homogenisation migrated to other building types, from public to private spaces.

The combination of optimised monofunctional elements or subsystems together with homogenised comfort zones very often requires an abundance of heating, cooling, air conditioning, ventilation, lighting and servicing equipment. While capital energy, embodied in the materials and building processes, might be kept fairly low, operational energy required for the running of a building is extremely high. Unfortunately, environmental design and engineering remains a question of post-design optimisation rather than informing the design process from a very early stage. Moreover, a homogenised interior environment simply cannot satisfy the multiple and contrasting needs of its inhabitants.

A remedy may be found in an understanding of architecture as ecology, involving dynamic and varied relations and mutual modulation between material systems, macro- and micro-environmental conditions, and individual and collective inhabitation. The proposed approach to architectural design is based on the deliberate differentiation of material systems and assemblies beyond the established catalogue of types, on making them dissimilar or distinct in degree and across ranges. Varied ranges of material systems can provide for diverse spatial arrangements together with climatic intensities. This involves the deployment of the inherent behavioural characteristics and modulation capacities of building elements and systems, rather than a retrospective optimisation process towards monofunctional efficiency. From this arises an understanding of efficiency as a dynamic characteristic of the effective, based on utilising redundancy predominantly as latent capacity to perform a series of different tasks, rather than a safety measure.

Instrumentalising multiple-performance capacity requires an understanding of material elements and systems in a synergetic and integral manner. It considers these systems in terms of their behavioural characteristics and capacities with respect to the purpose they serve locally and within the behavioural economy of larger systems. Today's so-called sustainable design claims this understanding, but operates on it mainly as a question of energy consumption, material lifecycles and waste production. An instrumental approach to relational behavioural characteristics as a way of modulating spaces and environments, however, requires operative retooling for architects with respect to analytical and generative methods and techniques and their relation and phasing within the design process.

Such an approach can benefit from learning from living nature, particularly the fact that most biological systems are articulated through higher-level multifunctional integration across at least eight scales of magnitude. This allows scale-dependent and scale-interdependent hierarchical and multiple functionality. In addition, architects can learn from connections and transitions between systems and subsystems of biological entities. In the building sector, connections between parts and elements are almost always discontinuous and articulated as dividing seams, instead of a smoother transition in materiality and thus functionality (such as can be seen in the way tendon and bone connect, deploying the same fibre material yet across a smooth transition of mineralisation). The understanding and deployment of gradient thresholds in materiality and environmental conditions can yield the potential for complex performance capacities of material systems. This will require a detailed understanding of the relation between material make-up and resultant behavioural characteristics.

Approaching material systems as a way of deploying behavioural characteristics and tendencies in an instrumental manner requires analytical methods, skills and tools with respect to the performance capacity of the overall system under investigation, and the narrower capacities of local elements that enable the global system to unfold its wider capacities.[5] What is needed is an approach to design that strongly integrates analytical and generative methods. Analysis is of central importance to the entire generative process not only in revealing behavioural and self-organisational tendencies, but also in assessing and designing spatial-environmental modulation capacity. In so doing, feedback between stimuli and responses and the conditioning relation between constraint and capacity will become the operative elements of heterogeneous spatial organisation. This suggests an architecture that modulates specified ranges and gradient conditions across space and over time, and that is based on strategically nested capacities within the material systems that make up the built environment. Such an approach to architectural design merges the tradition of substantial structures with that of ephemeral spaces and gradient thresholds towards complex performance capacity of the built environment.

The following projects pursue different methods of differentiating material systems, as researched by Michael Hensel and Achim Menges within OCEAN NORTH and the academic context of Diploma Unit 4 at the Architectural Association in London. Daniel Coll I Capdevila's Strip Morphologies deploys a bottom-up approach from a simple building element and its behaviour towards a differentiated assembly and its performance capacity. Neri Oxman's Vertical Helix introduces an integral approach to differentiating systems across a range of scales based on combined extensive scripting, modelling and analysis. And OCEAN NORTH's Jyväskylä Music and Art Centre pursues an iterative growth process based on multiple-performance systems towards a heterogeneous and dynamically modulated space.

Notes
1. Reyner Banham, *The Architecture of the Well-Tempered Environment*, University of Chicago Press (Chicago, IL), 1973.
2. Ibid, p 20.
3. Ibid.
4. See John Pile, *Open Office Planning*, The Architectural Press (London), 1978. See also Branden Hookway, *Pandemonium: The Rise of Predatory Locales in the Postwar World*, Princeton Architectural Press (Princeton, NJ), 1999.
5. Evolutionary biology can provide some useful analytical methods for this purpose. See Robert Cummings, 'Functional analysis', *Journal of Philosophy*, 72, 1975, pp 741–65.

Daniel Coll I Capdevila, Strip Morphologies, AA Diploma Unit 4 Design Study for Environmentally Differentiated Healing Environments, London, 2004–05

Spaces for healing environments are usually poorly designed homogeneous environments that are disadvantageous for the recovery of patients. However, individual needs and preferences of patients in the recovery period vary greatly, including ranges of privacy and exposure to light, sounds, temperature and airflow. This project therefore focuses on the development of a multi-performance material system with the capacity to provide for different spatial arrangements and to modulate the environment.

The selected material element is simple: steel strips cut from sheet material. Form-finding through bending and twisting enabled a systematic study of geometric behaviour. The derived geometric logic informed the definition of a digital element that integrates material characteristics, manufacturing constraints (the planar cutting from sheet material) and a related assembly logic. The digital parametric element comprises sets of geometric association that remain invariant within a defined range of transformations, ensuring

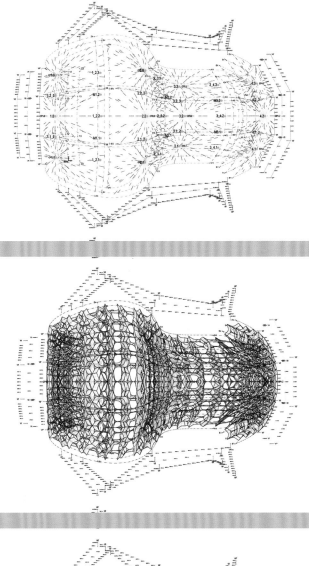

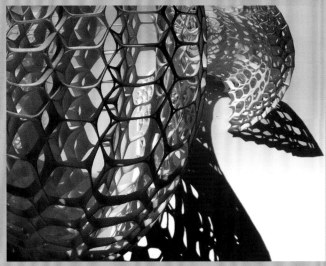

View of a rapid prototype model (selective laser sintering) showing one instance of a global configuration of the strip system, together with its specific modulation of light penetration and shadow casting.

A parametrically derived strip system. Top: Global surface geometry with tangency control framework. Middle: Corresponding population of digital strip components. Bottom: Curvature analysis of resultant strip morphology.

that any derived arrangement of strips can be directly fabricated and assembled.

Three strips were combined into a basic component for the digital and material system. The connection between the three strips that define the component is characterised by areas of tangency alignment, which introduces an additional control parameter that defines the orientation of the strip faces. These control points, together with arrays of points defined by the u/v parameterisation of notional control surfaces, provided the geometric setup for the population of a larger system. Proliferation entails that the parametrically defined components populate a larger system by adapting their specific geometric articulation to it. Each local component is differentiated by adjacent components, the global geometry of the control surface and external control points.

Establishing the system as an associative geometric framework in a parametric modelling application delivers various levels of control to the designer. On the local scale the width and thickness of the steel strips can be changed and the orientation of each strip can be altered. On a regional system scale the density of strips can be changed, and on a global system scale the geometric and topo[...] articulation of the entire system can be manipulated. Apart from modifications derived by changing the parametric variables of the system, the underlying geometric aspects of the system can be altered and redefined too.

This setup enables the designer to implement complex changes to the system instantaneously. Digital simulation of the system's capacity to modulate the luminous and sonic environment and its visual transparency serves to analyse and compare different instances of system articulation towards their performance capacities. The ability to achieve and evaluate system performance across multiple variations accelerates the feedback between analysis and design evolution. In this way, a material system can be devised for the improvement of healing environments or other programmes that are context-sensitive with respect to given spatial constraints and environmental input. Thus the desired ranges of spatial organisation and environmental modulation can be achieved through a rigorous, iterative and swift, thus economical, design process.

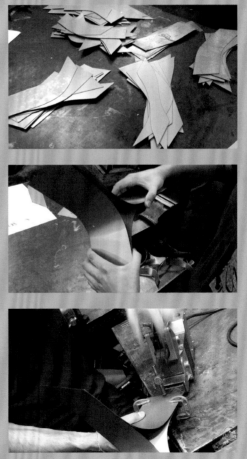

Production of a full-scale prototype. Left: Partial prototype. Right, top to bottom: Laser-cut steel strips, tangency alignment of strips, and spot welding of the aligned strips.

Neri Oxman, Performative Morphologies:
The Vertical Helix, AA Diploma Unit 4 Design Study for a
New High-Rise Morphology, London, 2003−04

Performative morphologies are derived from a condition-based design process. Design is generated or modulated by condition statements and requirements. These can be intrinsic (for example, programmatic related circulation) or extrinsic to the designed system (such as environmental conditions). This project aimed at developing design methods that are conditioned by multivariant influences, and utilises specific attributes of helical morphologies in order to achieve spatial, organisational and performative differentiation.

Neri Oxman deployed a helical morphology for the differentiation of vertical structures and buildings, and instrumentalises geometric and structural characteristics from local component to overall building scale. The morphology distributes loads over its envelope, facilitated by a hybrid structure that combines the vectorial load path of a linear component with the field distribution of a structural surface. The load paths are treated differentially, with loads being bundled along vectors where necessary and distributed across surfaces wherever possible and useful, towards embedding latent capacities that can compensate for local disruptions to the structural systems. In addition, circulation is not limited to service cores. Instead, it is distributed across a multitude of helical paths, providing for different spatial experiences and evacuation routes.

A rigorous toolset was developed that can facilitate the design process towards morphological differentiation through scripting and parametric applications. Digital tools were customised to fit the characteristics of helical arrangements in terms of geometric articulation. Modelling in Rhinoceros, in combination with Excel scripting, served to derive different instances of geometric articulations of the system. This approach is neither top-down, from an

Geometrical studies of the different generic types of global-scale helical configurations. Five basic geometrical curves were scripted to produce geometrical variation by merging and/or changing the mathematical data in a systematic manner.

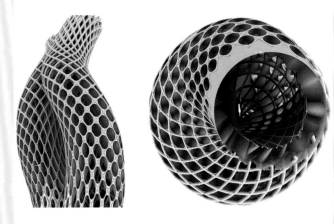

Digital model of the entire structure (isometric and top views). The structure comprises an external and an internal surface connected by a cellular fabric acting as a differentiated structural skin element. Cell depth and thickness are modulated according to structural performance and spatial criteria.

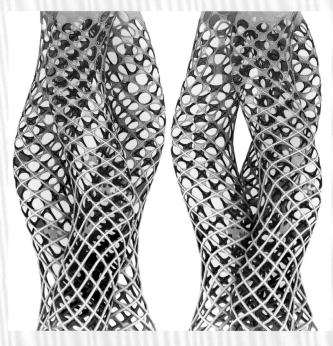

Digital image (two elevation views) of the structural skin developed as a bundled structure. A composite-based system combining the structural strands with additional surface members is articulated to create a structurally differentiated envelope in which force flows are distributed along its entire surface.

overall geometry to detailed local articulation, nor bottom-up, from a defined component or local articulation to the overall system.

The specific helical arrangement was developed in all relevant system scales simultaneously. In doing so, Bentley Systems' GenerativeComponents, among other software packages, was used to establish a relational geometric logic by which different instances of geometric articulation can more easily be derived though a parametric setup and modification. The evaluation of the structural performance of different geometric articulations integrated physical and digital methods. Scaled physical models were evaluated by applying loads to register the resultant displacement on a local, regional and global system scale. Digital analysis based on the finite element method enabled the determination of stresses and displacement.

An analytical approach was developed that synthesised geometric and structural data, derived from the bending, buckling and torque behaviour of the system. The results of the structural behaviour analysis informed each stage of the iterative design process.

Spatial arrangement and circulatory organisation was evaluated in parallel. Intersecting surfaces that connect the various helical paths result in the formation of spatial pockets. Circulation paths follow the helical arrangement and interconnect spatial pockets. Parametric changes to the system affect the location, size and orientation of spatial pockets towards environmental input, such as daylight and thermal exposure. This was analysed through digital simulation, and informed the iterative design process. In this way, design generation and analysis went hand in hand, with each instance of the project development becoming increasingly informed by context-specific stimuli.

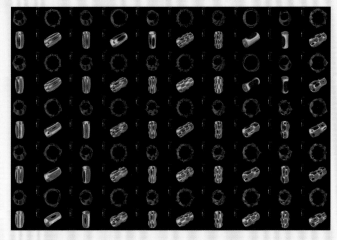

Each of the 480 registered tiles is defined by its geometry, its surface area, and its stress condition across a geometrically idealised map of the unrolled configurations (top). The periodic nonuniform tiling was applied to the skin by projecting the uniform skin elements onto the nonuniform global body. Shades of grey correspond to the relative location of each of the 16 strands comprising the entire volume (bottom).

Linear finite element analysis (FEA): static structural analysis of a local cylindrical patch performed in consecutive buckling modes under applied vertical load. The analysis determines the relationship between the mechanical properties of the surface and the load applied. Each mode represents one behavioural instance in the process of load application and is assessed by the nature of the buckling patterns that appear on the surface as a response to a given load case.

OCEAN NORTH, Jyväskylä Music and Art Centre Phase 02 and 03 Design Study, London, 2004–05

The project aimed for a differentiated event space and an extension of the landscaped town square into an acoustically animated interior landscape that caters for formal symphonic and orchestral events and art exhibitions, as well as for informal cultural activities. The lattice structure and surfaces that articulate the interior provide for ad-hoc stages, and seating and exhibition areas, while creating a dynamically articulated space of acoustic and visual intensities, with the lattices being locally sound-active.[1] This extends acoustic experience beyond the interior of the music hall and rehearsal rooms into the interior landscape of the building volume. The layered envelope consists of a transparent and reflective skin. Exterior and interior light conditions affect the layered gradients of reflection and transparency, which yield the perception of a boundless deep space. Directionality, density and layering of the lattices, and the surfaces and volumes that evolve from it, result in the perception of a locally differentiated yet vast space.

OCEAN NORTH deployed an iterative growth process that articulates the lattices, informed by rules pertaining to i) the location, orientation and density of the struts that make up the lattice systems; ii) structural, sonic and luminous performance requirements; iii) spatial design guidelines. The resulting lattice systems inform the geometries of the terrain, structure and envelopes of primary and secondary spaces and surface areas, circulation pattern and the sound-active system.

The growth process commenced from the definition and distribution of virtual volumes informed by the programmatic requirements of the project brief. A series of gradient maps organised along the x, y and z planes that delimit the growth area for the various lattice systems inform the growth process with performative requirements. Such maps constrain the local search space for each strut of the lattice system in terms of size and search angle. For this project the gradient maps are based on structural performance, as well as the modulation of the luminous and sonic microenvironments of the interstitial space between the outer envelope of the building and the envelopes of the various spaces not to be intersected by the lattice system. Subsequently, a first set of definition points and search rules are defined that distribute and orientate the struts that make

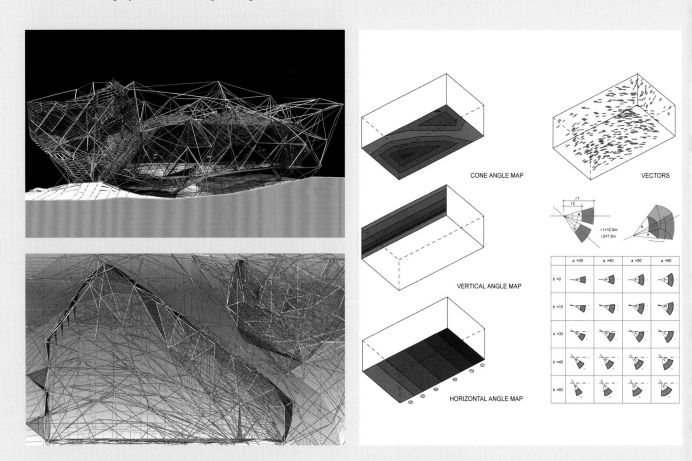

View of model scale 1:75 showing the primary, secondary and tertiary lattice systems without the building envelope (top), and plan view of the centre showing the primary, secondary and tertiary lattice systems and the volumes of the music hall and the rehearsal rooms (bottom).

Diagrams showing the strategic constraints of the growth process, including the local search windows that determine the angles of each strut of the lattice in relation to the connection with the neighbouring struts (right), as well as the gradient maps that allocate search-window constraints to regions within the building envelope (left).

up the primary lattice system in response to the above outlined rule set. From the primary system, a second set of virtual surfaces is derived on which a new set of definition points is defined. In further iterations, secondary and tertiary lattice systems are evolved that define mesh-like enclosures for the required internal volumes, circulation and sound-active systems.

While the iterative growth process is informed by performance requirements, the synergetic impact of the various systems working together needs nevertheless to be analysed in stages. Digital structural and luminous performance analysis was conducted repeatedly in order to evaluate the emerging conditions and synergies between the various systems that make up the project.

From the differential density and angular variation of the lattice systems, and the varied distribution of sound-active elements, evolves a spatial and ambient differentiation of the scheme: a heterogeneous space in which augmented spatial and ambient differentiation provide for choices between microenvironmental conditions that can provide for the time-specific individual requirements of inhabitants. Δ

Note
1. See Natasha Barett's and OCEAN NORTH's Agora project, a sound-active installation in Michael Hensel, 'Digital architectures: Are we ready to compute?', in Neil Leach, David Turnbull and Chris Williams (eds), *Digital Tectonics*, Wiley-Academy (Chichester), 2004, pp 120–6.

Project credits
Phase 01 (1997): Kivi Sotamaa, Johan Bettum, Markus Holmstén and Kim Baumann Larsen with Lasse Wagner, Vesa Oiva, and Hein van Dam.
Phase 02 (2004): Michael Hensel, Achim Menges and Kivi Sotamaa with Hani Fallaha, Shireen Han, Andrew Kudless, Neri Oxman, Nazaneen Roxanne Shafaie, Cordula Stach, Nikolaos Stathopoulos, Mark Tynan and Muchuan Xu.
Phase 03 (2005–06): Michael Hensel and Achim Menges with Nikolaos Stathopoulos.

Morphogenetic growth process. Top to bottom: Distribution of seed and definition points for the struts of the primary lattice system; first growth step of the primary lattice system; growth step defining the secondary lattice system in accordance with the primary system; model view of the same location

Manufacturing Diversity

Recent developments of digital fabrication and computer-aided manufacturing (CAM) in the building sector have a profound impact on architecture as a material practice. In this article, **Achim Menges** describes advanced processes of steel, timber and membrane fabrication and construction through an investigation of the pioneering work of world-leading manufacturing companies Covertex, Finnforest Merk, Octatube Space Structures, Seele and Skyspan.

Covertex, pneumatic cladding installation for the Allianz Arena, Munich, Germany, 2004.

Architecture as a material practice is changing rapidly through the increasing number of geometrically complex designs accomplished by leading practices, and through a growing interest in a built environment that is becoming much more diverse than in the days of mass production and standardisation of building elements and systems. The key concepts underlying these developments are, for example, variation or differentiation leading to varied building elements and systems that are similar in degree, together with an increasingly integral relation between building systems and elements that are different in kind.

The work of leading manufacturing companies in the building sector confirms the contemporary belief that computer-aided manufacturing (CAM) processes are playing a critical role in a potential paradigm shift from mass production and its inherent standardisation, to the conception and production of differentiated building elements and systems. Thus it seems to be critical now to understand digital production as a strategic aspect of the design process rather than a merely facilitative activity; especially as CAM is not at all a recent technological development.

Initially developed with the support of the US military to overcome the limitations of mechanised mass production in the 1950s, the first generation of computer-controlled automation introduced numerical control (NC) to machines for metalworking applications. Over the following four decades, derivate systems, now referred to as computer numerical control (CNC), have been developed for a much wider range of materials and a variety of scales, and still constitute the basis for most CAM applications. The arrival of microprocessors in the 1970s, the development of personal computers (PCS) in the 1980s, and the associated proliferation of desktop computing and related use of computer-aided design (CAD) applications, had profound effects on the dissemination of CAM.

The resulting transfer and integration of digital manufacturing and its increasing affordability has begun to significantly transform the building industry. The seemingly contradictory ambition of differentiation and economy of designers and manufacturers alike is becoming resolved by the transformation of mass customisation from a futuristic goal to a realistic approach. A diverse range of current and emergent digital-manufacturing processes, related facilitating expertise, enabling technology and construction strategies for the production task of complex building designs is currently being explored by world-leading companies. These processes do not only give an insight into what is possible to construct today, but help outline the potentialities inherent in advanced manufacturing and fabrication for future tectonic possibilities in architectural design.

Octatube Space Structures: Computer-Aided Composite Sandwich Manufacturing and Explosive Panel Forming

Octatube Space Structures, based in Delft in the Netherlands, has been exploring innovative means of digital production enabled and supported by advanced digital design and engineering approaches for more than a decade. Such innovation has been driven and consolidated by working on various prominent building projects, one of which is the Municipial Floriade Pavilion, called Hydra Pier, in Hoofddorp, a competition-winning design of Asymptote Architects.

Octatube was contracted for the construction of the pavilion's curved-glass facade, a water-filled suspended frameless glass pond and the double-curved roof panels of the building. The curved-glass facade was constructed as a combination of hot-bent monolithic glass panels and cold-bent panels that achieve a camber of 80 millimetres (3 inches) over a 2-metre (6.5-foot) side length. The glass pond of 5 by 12 metres (16 x 39 feet) was articulated as suspended polygonal flat panels made from fully prestressed glass. However, the

Explosive forming at the premises of Exploform in Delft (top left); Negative fibre-reinforced concrete moulds formed on positive CNC-milled polystyrene moulds (top right); resulting double-curved aluminium panel with welded aluminium edges (left).

Octatube double-curved aluminium panels
Test assembly of panels on wooden jig (top left), and finished panels on Hydra Pier roof (top right); Exterior view of the Hydra Pier project in Hoofddorp, the Netherlands, designed by Asymptote Architects, 2002 (left).

Left: Octatube GRP/PIR polyurethane sandwich construction CNC-milled polystyrene mould for a roof segment at Holland Composites in Lelystad (top), and vacuum injection of the first polyester layer eventually becoming part of the roof surface (bottom); Middle: Transportation of the Octatube Yitzak Rabin Center library roof segments in special containers from Lelystad to Tel Aviv (top) and assembly of the lower library roof structure onsite in Israel (bottom); Right: Roof structures of the Yitzak Rabin Center, Tel Aviv, designed by Moshe Safdie Architects, 2005.

main challenge proved to be the manufacturing and assembly of the double-curved panels of the roof cladding.

With only one axis of symmetry in the freeform roof geometry, Octatube had to develop a process of fabricating a range of 3-D panels from aluminium sheets that are considerably different in size, curvature and depth. In order to achieve this variation in the double-curved geometry of the panels, the company developed a combined process of digital production and explosive forming. Explosive forming as such is not an entirely new method. It was first documented in 1888 for the engraving of iron plates and has been used in the aerospace industry for the manufacture of complex short-production-run components such as curved domes of missiles and rocket nose cones since the 1950s. Explosive forming entails the forcing of sheet metal into dies and moulds through the detonation of explosives under water. In a water tank the metal sheet to be formed is placed on top of the mould and sealed, and a vacuum in the mould cavity is produced. Due to the noncompressible nature of water, the pressure load of the detonating explosive located on top of the metal is relatively evenly distributed and forces the sheet into the mould. The vacuum ensures complete alignment of material and mould surface in the forming process.

Similar to many other fabrication processes of the aerospace industry, explosive forming proved to be too expensive for use in the building industry. However, Octatube, in collaboration with the Dutch company Exploform, has managed to adapt this process to an economically feasible production of cladding panels through the integration of advanced CAM. The required negative moulds were articulated by casting fibre-reinforced concrete into positive moulds, all of which were CNC milled from solid polystyrene blocks hardened with epoxy-resin glass. The necessary numeric data for the manufacturing of the geometry of each panel was extracted directly from the digital 3-D model of the pavilion roof.

Due to the strict government restrictions regarding the use of explosives, the actual forming process took place in water tanks at the premises of Exploform in Delft. The achieved geometric precision was demonstrated by the remarkable side effect that even the intricate tessellation of the original digital model, which is registered in the CAM process and thus expressed in the manufactured object, could still be recognised on the formed panels. The panels were then assembled on a wooden jig that had also been CNC cut using the data from the digital 3-D model. On this jig, digitally cut aluminium strips were welded onto the edges of the panels to allow for a watertight assembly using 10-millimetre (0.4-inch) gaskets at the seams between the panels. After spray painting, in order to achieve a durable and smooth surface finish, the complex 3-D aluminium panels were ready for assembly on the Floriade Pavilion roof.

In a subsequent project, Octatube explored an alternative way of constructing a smooth double-curved roof structure. The design of the Yitzak Rabin Center in Tel Aviv, Israel, by architect Moshe Safdie features five distinct double-curved roof surfaces over two building parts – the library and the great hall. Initially these roof surfaces were planned as steel structures with concrete cladding, but Octatube developed an alternative stressed-skin construction during the tender period. The concept challenged the original distinction of a load-bearing primary structure and cladding system by proposing a self-supporting polystyrene shell wrapped in glass-fibre-reinforced polyester layers. In this way, Octatube explored a different approach to constructing double-curved surfaces, namely by investigating the possibilities of deploying CNC-milled polystyrene as the load-bearing structure instead of using it as a mould, as in the Floriade Pavilion project. The proposed structures, not dissimilar to large surfboards, were approved by the client and architect, and Octatube was commissioned to engineer and build the five roofs.

The complex geometry, the considerable span of up to 30 x 20 metres (98 x 66 feet) and the 8-metre (26-foot) long cantilevering wing tips prone to fatigue due to changing wind loads presented a major technical challenge. Nonetheless, Octatube managed to stay relatively close to its initial concept in the eventual realisation of the project. The roof geometry was divided into 2.5-metre (8-foot) wide strips and digitally produced from Octatube's 3-D model. Complot BV in Delft, which had already cooperated with Octatube in the Floriade project, machined polystyrene blocks into the required mould shapes by CNC milling. The moulds were delivered to another company, Holland Composites, where they were then covered with a special foil. A thick layer of coating and glass-fibre mats was applied on the negative moulds, and the glass fibre was impregnated with polyester resin using vacuum injection. After this layer had hardened, fire-resistant PIR polyurethane blocks were sawn, applied and covered with another layer of glass-fibre mats. The resulting roof segments are 30 millimetres (1.2 inches) thick and wrapped in 7-millimetre (0.3-inch) thick glass-fibre-reinforced vinylester resin. Internal GRP stringers reinforce the shell structure and cope with the forces introduced by the supporting columns as well as preventing the top and bottom GRP layers from delaminating.

The integrated working methods of Octatube allowed the utilisation of a digital master model to facilitate all engineering tasks and subsequent 'file-to-factory' production. The 3-D model also provided the relevant data to plan the efficient transport of the roof segments, which were nested in special containers and shipped from the Netherlands to Israel. Onsite in Tel Aviv, the five load-bearing stressed-skin sandwich shells were then assembled, glued together by additional seam reinforcements and wrapped in a final GRP layer.

Octatube's developments for the Floriade Pavilion and Rabin Center roof structures indicate how an integrated approach to computer-aided design and manufacturing enables the fabrication and construction of geometrically complex building surfaces. In addition to this, digital production has also opened up new possibilities for the manufacturing of building systems that may consist of several thousand geometrically different components, as demonstrated by Covertex's pneumatic cladding system for the Allianz Arena in Munich.

Covertex and Skyspan: Digitally Driven Membrane Engineering and Fabrication

In 2003, Covertex, a German company specialising in membrane constructions, was commissioned to realise the pneumatic roof and facade system of Herzog & de Meuron's competition-winning proposal for a new soccer stadium, the Allianz Arena, in Munich. This entailed the planning and construction of approximately 26,000 square metres (280,000 square feet) of facade area and 38,000 square metres (409,000 square feet) of roof area consisting of 2816 individual rhomboid double-layered air-filled cushions, all of which needed to be defined and the related cutting patterns generated. Each cushion is manufactured from ethylen-tetrafluorethylen (ETFE), either transparent, or with gradient

translucent print patterns, attached to the supporting transom steel structure, individually inflated and equipped with a drainage pipe penetrating the upper cushion surface to avoid heavy water accumulation in the case of accidental deflation.

The different cushion geometries meant that the gradient print patterns and the drainage hole, to be situated at the lowest point after an eventual collapse, also needed to be individually specified for each element. In addition, all cushion surfaces, with a diagonal length of up to 16 metres (52 feet), needed to be welded together from 1.5-metre (5-foot) wide ETFE rolls. The resulting complexity involved in the design, logistics and manufacturing compelled Covertex to use advanced CAD/CAM techniques and technologies for the form-finding and production process of the membrane structures. The architect's digital model, which defined just the construction lines, served as a base for Covertex's subsequent engineering process. A custom-made software tool allowed automated tracing of all relevant coordinate points in the architect's model and notating them in spreadsheets. Additional programmed routines generated the precise offset of supporting frames and defined the associated attachment points of each cushion. These points then enabled the digital form-finding of the inflated state of each cushion and the subsequent generation of each cutting pattern, including the relevant coordinate

Skyspan PTFE fibreglass fabric manufacturing. Fabric check on light table (top), computer-controlled cutting (centre), and high-temperature welding of PTFE fabric (bottom).

Views of Skyspan retractable PVC/PES-coated PVC fabric roof of the Commerzbank Arena, Frankfurt, designed by Gerkan Mark & Partner Architects, 2005.

Exterior view of the Allianz Arena, Munich, designed by Herzog & de Meuron, 2004

information, the position of the cut lines and overlapping welding seams, the related orientation of the gradient print pattern and the location of the air supply and drainage holes.

The resulting datasets permitted the direct cutting and labelling of all ETFE elements by a digitally controlled cutting and marking machine at KfM in Germany. Subsequently, a digitally controlled welder connected the foil strips of each cushion, producing more than 250 kilometres (155 miles) of weld lines in the process. The limits of this technology became apparent due to the necessity of manually detailing the corner points of each cushion. However, the extensive use of integrated CAD/CAM enabled Covertex to realise the entire 64,000 square metres (689,000 square feet) of pneumatic cladding system, including all partial tasks such as calculation of the cutting patterns of the cushions, cushion manufacturing, production of fixation profiles, sealing, ventilation and air supply systems within a period of just 15 months.

In addition to air-inflated cushion systems, another versatile membrane construction for covering large and geometrically complex roof structures is mechanically pretensioned foil and fabric systems, as demonstrated in Skyspan's stadium roof in Frankfurt. The design of the new Commerzbank Arena by

Gerkan Mark & Partner features the world's largest retractable PVC cover, at 9600 square metres (103,000 square feet), and an 18,000-square-metre (194,000-square-foot) large membrane roof made from PTFE fibreglass fabric. While ETFE is a homogeneous foil, PTFE is a fibreglass fabric with anisotropic behaviour in warp and weft direction and with irregularities resulting from the weaving process. For this reason, Skyspan, a German specialist in membrane constructions, tests patches of each fabric production run on a digital biaxial measuring machine. After several test cycles the measurement data is fed back to the engineer to inform the digital form-finding process of the particular project geometry.

During this process, a fundamental understanding of the material behaviour and characteristics is as important as comprehensive digital tools. Once the pretensioned shape of the membrane construction had been form-found, the subsequent digital pattern generation was informed by the material anisotropy and took the necessary oversize for welding seams into account. After checking and marking local irregularities on the PTFE fabric on a light table, the generated patterns were nested on the material roll and cut into segments by a digitally controlled plotter. High-temperature welding was used to

Covertex computer-aided ETFE membrane manufacturing. Digitally controlled cutting and marking of ETFE foil (left and centre) and computer-aided membrane welding at KfM in Germany (right).

connect the PTFE segments. The final pretensioning of the outer PTFE roof took place during the assembly process.

The inner retractable stadium roof, made from PVC/PES-coated PVC fabric, required a substantial belt system to withstand rain and wind loads. A new self-driving sewing machine was developed for the differential pretensioning of the belts during the process of stitching them together. This new manufacturing method, combined with digital simulations and exact calculations of the belts' and PVC's prestress, ensured that the retractable roof could be built and is now working.

Seele: Integrated CAD/CAM Steel and Glass Facade Construction

Due to the inherent flexibility of membranes, the main challenge for advanced foil and fabric constructions lies within the enhanced integration of digital design, form-finding and pattern generation and computer-aided processes of analysing, cutting and welding the material. In comparison, the fabrication and construction of building skins made from more rigid materials such as metal and glass require a greater range of digital forming and fabrication processes. Seele, a leading company in the design, engineering and construction of bespoke glass facade systems, employs a wide range of different CAD/CAM processes.

At its main manufacturing facility, situated right next to its engineering offices in southern Germany, Seele utilises computer-controlled machines for most cladding production tasks. Metal and aluminium profiles are cut by a numerically controlled saw permitting the rapid production of different length workpieces. A special CNC drilling and welding unit facilitates the preparation of holes and the fixation of stud poles according to digitally defined distance and angle protocols. Sheet material is automatically allocated, prepared, cut and marked by a digitally controlled laser. The laser is a powerful and controllable source of thermal energy that enables the cutting and marking of sheet material to any shape within the constraints of the machine. At Seele's factory, the laser is combined with a digitally controlled shelving system that automatically selects, prepares and positions the material on the laser bed to increase workflow efficiency. Another machine facilitates the CNC bending and folding of sheet metal materials.

Finnforest Merk 3-D curved timber tracks. Basic gluelam arches (left) prepared for subsequent robotic milling (centre); finished 3-D curved timber tracks installed on a wooden rollercoaster in Soltau, Germany (right).

Finnforest Merk Serpentine Pavilion timber structure. Robotic manufacturing of timber elements (left); mock-up of lattice elements joined by mortice-and-tenon connections (centre); installation of timber structure onsite in London (right).

These CAM facilities, combined with sophisticated solid modelling CAD applications, allow for consistent engineering and fabrication datasets that have enabled Seele to contribute to the production of highly complex buildings such as the Seattle Central Library designed by OMA. In this project, Seele was responsible for the cladding preconstruction services, the production and installation of the 11,900 square metres (128,000 square feet) of exterior cladding comprising more than 6500 glass panels and 30,000 anodised aluminium profiles. The building's faceted skin geometry required extensive 3-D engineering as the facade surfaces of aluminium extrusions, silicone gaskets, triple-glazing panels, pressure plates, gutters and closing panels join in up to five different angles at particular node points. A comprehensive digital 3-D solid model of the entire facade provided the manufacturing data for all prefabricated elements as well as the related labelling information, packing lists and transportation schedules.

The digital model also allowed for adjusting the production and installation of the facade system to tolerances in the primary steelwork of up to 2.5 centimetres (1 inch) occurring after the actual erection. For these adjustments a digital scanning process notates clusters of measure points of the already built primary structure in relation to fixed reference points. The resulting 3-D point cloud allows for digitally overlapping the primary system as built with the digital model of the facade as designed. The identified deviations can then be compensated for in the manufacturing and installation of the cladding elements on site.

Finnforest Merk: Robotic Timber Manufacturing

Most of the CAM processes described thus far require specialised machines that can perform specific manufacturing tasks such as milling, cutting, welding and so on. However, in a few cases the more versatile machines used, for instance, in the automotive industry are beginning to be employed in the building industry. An interesting example of this development is the use of a robotic manufacturing unit by German timber construction company Finnforest Merk. Equipped with different tool heads and driven by the appropriate software, such a basic manufacturing robot can execute diverse manufacturing processes ranging from welding of sheet metal to cutting and sewing of composite reinforcement. Furthermore, such robots can automatically identify the position and type of workpiece to be machined, perform an entire sequence of fabrication steps by automatically changing tool heads, and later on check the result for accuracy and tolerances.

Equipping such a basic robotic unit for timber manufacturing has enabled Finnforest Merk to produce both complex single building elements and geometrically complex constructions made from a large number of different components. A typical case for the fabrication of complex building elements is the 3-D curved timber tracks Merk produced for a wooden rollercoaster located in Soltau in Germany. For this project, Merk combined its long-established expertise in producing gluelam arches with the machining potential of its five-axis robot equipped with a milling tool and the ability of its CAD/CAM engineers to translate the relevant data into machine-readable manufacturing protocols. The high strength required by cars travelling at 120 kilometres (75 miles) per hour and forces of up to 4g, as well as the complex curvature of the tracks, was achieved by robotically machining gluelam arches curved in one plane into 3-D curved beams.

In another project, the 2005 Serpentine Pavilion designed by Álvaro Siza and Eduardo Souto de Moura together with Cecil Balmond of Arup and Partners, the main challenge for Merk has been the construction of a complex structure from a large number of unique components. The pavilion's 17-metre (56-foot) clear spanning curved roof and walls are articulated as an undulating offset grid of laminated timber. The lattice elements are arranged in mutually supporting patterns and joined by mortice-and-tenon connections. The unique geometry of each element was digitally defined by Arup's Advanced Geometry Unit and mapped out in a format that could directly communicate with Finnforest Merk's CAD/CAM engineers. Using robot technology the required 427 unique timber beams could be manufactured within two weeks. Starting at one corner and radiating out to the opposite sides, the subsequent assembly process of the lattice also required a specific protocol defining the only possible erection sequence for the unique interlocking beams.

Today, with digital production and continuous datasets comprising a practical approach rather than an idealised aim, the production of geometrically complex buildings and building systems from differentiated components appears a tangible, as well as feasible, proposition. Overall, the most relevant consideration for now is the relation between existing skills and tools and emerging techniques and technologies. The work of the leading manufacturing companies suggests that the transfer and integration of CAM in the field of construction requires the development of new production approaches in parallel with an understanding of

traditional means and skills. In fact, CAD/CAM technology may become a mechanism through which the potential of existing expertise and methods is fully realised. The projects and processes that have been presented here indicate that the critical moment of integrating existing and emerging manufacturing techniques and technologies provides the inroad into an understanding of the yet uncovered potential of new means of digital production. This moment of synthesis and synergy will be the vehicle for rethinking in the necessary and latent redefinition of the construction process itself. ⊅

This article is based on an indepth research into the current possibilities and future perspectives of fully integrated computer-aided design and manufacturing. As part of this exploration, Achim Menges and Michael Hensel visited specialist manufacturing companies and their facilities in Germany to investigate and discuss the latest computer-controlled fabrication processes. Following this field trip, the Emergence and Design Group organised the symposium entitled 'Manufacturing Diversity', with representatives of the key companies at the Architectural Association in February 2005. The article reports on the work and projects presented by Dirk Emmer (Skyspan, Germany), Benoit Fauchon (Covertex, Germany), Michael Keller (Finnforest Merk, Germany), Thomas Spitzer (Seele, Germany) and Dr Karel Vollers representing Professor Mick Eekhout (Octatube, the Netherlands).

Interior view of the Serpentine Pavilion designed by Álvaro Siza and Eduardo Souto de Moura together with Cecil Balmond of Arup and Partners, London, 2005.

Polymorphism

Achim Menges presents a range of morphogenetic design techniques and technologies that synthesise processes of formation and materialisation. Through a series of design experiments, he explains his research into an understanding of form, materials and structure, not as separate elements, but rather as complex interrelations in polymorphic systems resulting from the response to varied input and environmental influences, and derived through the logics of advanced manufacturing processes.

Natural morphogenesis, the process of evolutionary development and growth, generates polymorphic systems that obtain their complex organisation and shape from the interaction of system-intrinsic material capacities and external environmental influences and forces. The resulting, continuously changing, complex structures are hierarchical arrangements of relatively simple material components organised through successive series of propagated and differentiated subassemblies from which the system's performative abilities emerge.

A striking aspect of natural morphogenesis is that formation and materialisation processes are always inherently and inseparably related. In stark contrast to these integral development processes of material form, architecture as a material practice is mainly based on design approaches that are characterised by a hierarchical relationship that prioritises the generation of form over its subsequent materialisation. Equipped with representational tools intended for explicit, scalar geometric descriptions, the architect creates a scheme through a range of design criteria that leave the inherent morphological and performative capacities of the employed material systems largely unconsidered. Ways of materialisation, production and construction are strategised and devised as top-down engineered, material solutions only after defining the shape of the building and the location of tectonic elements.

An alternative morphogenetic approach to architectural design entails unfolding morphological complexity and performative capacity from material constituents without differentiating between formation and materialisation processes. Over the last five years I have pursued related design research through projects and also in educational collaboration with various colleagues at the Architectural Association (AA) and other schools. Based on concepts of developmental biology and biomimetic engineering, the core of such a morphogenetic approach is an understanding of material systems not as derivatives of standardised building systems and elements facilitating the construction of pre-established design schemes, but rather as generative drivers in the design process.

Extending the concept of a material system by embedding its material characteristics, geometric behaviour, manufacturing constraints and assembly logics allows for deriving and elaborating a design through the system's intrinsic performative capacities. This promotes an understanding of form, materials and structure not as separate elements, but rather as complex interrelations in polymorphic systems resulting from the response to varied input and environmental influences and derived through the logics and constraints of advanced manufacturing processes. This demands new modes of integrating design techniques, production technologies and system performance, a cross-section of which will be discussed here. Through a series of five morphogenetic design experiments ranging from homologous systems[1] to polytypic species,[2] the characteristics of integral form-generation processes enabled through parametric association, differential actuation, dynamic relaxation, algorithmic definition and digital growth will be examined. Discussing the organisational potentialities and spatial opportunities that arise from such a design approach would go beyond the scope of this article.[3] The focus is therefore placed on presenting relevant tools and methods for such an integral approach to design.

Form-Finding and Dynamic Relaxation: Membrane Morphologies

The disconnection of form generation and subsequent materialisation emblematic for current design approaches manifests itself in the 'hard control' that the architect needs to exert on the constructs he or she designs. Before any material realisation can take place, the designer must define the precise location and exact shape of all elements, geometrically controlling the maximum amount of points needed to describe the system to be constructed. However, such a design method fails to notice the potential of using the capacity for self-organisation inherent to material systems. This suggests a design process based on the strategic 'soft control' of minimal definition that instrumentalises the behaviour of a material system in the formation process. Integrating the logics of form, material and structure was investigated in a series of membrane structures[4] developed by Michael Hensel and myself as exhibition installations for different locations. Membrane structures are of particular interest for such an exploration, as any resultant morphology is intrinsically related to the material characteristics and the formation process of pretensioning. Thus a viable design method cannot be based on geometric hard control over a maximum number of points of the system, but should be based on the local exertion of force on strategic points.

Form-finding, as pioneered by Frei Otto,[5] is a design technique that utilises the self-organisation of material systems under the influence of extrinsic forces. In membrane structures the displacement of particular boundary points and the consequent pretensioning force are correlated with the material and form, in that the form of the structure can be found as the state of equilibrium of internal resistances and external forces. Form-finding processes for membranes can be physically modelled and simulated through digital dynamic relaxation. The latter involves a digital mesh that settles into an equilibrium state through iterative calculations based on the specific elasticity and material make-up of the membrane – isotropic in case of foils, anisotropic in case of fabrics – combined with the designation of boundary points and related forces. The same software applications can usually also generate the associated cutting patterns if the membrane is to be constructed from relatively nonelastic material.

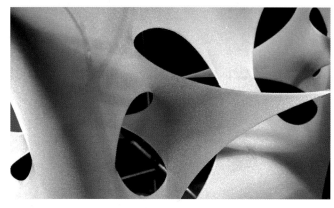

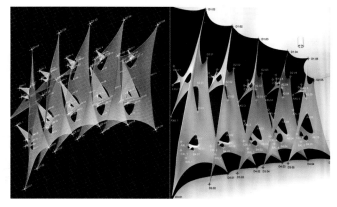

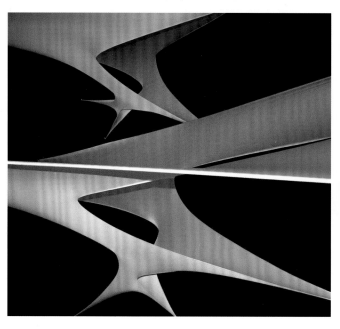

Form-finding and dynamic relaxation
Clockwise from top left: Initial form-finding experiment (top) and close-up view of 'minimal hole' configuration (bottom); 'Membrane Morphologies 02' installed at the Architectural Association, London; close-up view of

membrane installation resulting from parametrically defined patch specification, cut location and pretensioning action; digital model form found through dynamic relaxation processes (left) and related specification and installation of 'Membrane Morphologies 02' (right).

In the project presented here, the material consists of nylon fabric with different elasticity in the warp and weft direction. An additional design aspect was the introduction of holes cut into the fabric that considerably alter the behaviour of the membrane. These holes were critical as they expanded the performance range of the system. While traditional form-finding methods focus on structural behaviour of material form resulting in monoparametric assessment criteria, the aim of this project was the exploration of a multiparametric approach. Thus the additional capacity of the perforated membrane system to modulate visual permeability as a

differentiated exhibition screen was understood as being intrinsically related to the structural form. In order to instrumentalise this relation, two operations were of critical importance for the design process: first, the parametric specification and subsequent confection of each membrane patch defined by boundary points and cutting lines expressed within the object coordinate space of the patch and, second, the pretensioning action defined through the relocation of the object boundary points towards anchor points described in the coordinate space of the exhibition room. Feeding back information between examining different values of local

Differential surface actuation
Material prototype displaying curvature resulting from the differential fastening of 7680 actuator bolts.

parametric variables and testing altering positions for the anchor-point coordinates creates multiple membrane morphologies that all remain coherent with the construction logics of the system. A specific configuration can be developed through corroborating and negotiating different behavioural characteristics and specific performance requirements. The resulting membrane morphology settles into a stable state of unity between form and force. At the same time the correlated complex curvature of the membrane and the opening of the holes provide for different degrees of visual permeability resulting in the varied exposure of the exhibits.

Differential Surface Actuation: Metapatch Project

In most form-finding processes, operations focus on the exertion of force on strategic system-points, which leads to a 'global' manipulation of the overall system. In this context, 'global' refers to the entirety of a system, while 'local' describes a sublocation. It is important to realise that the self-organising capacity of material systems is not limited to 'global' form-finding processes such as the one mentioned above. It can also be deployed in a 'local' manner. One such exploration is the project developed by Joseph Kellner and David Newton[6] in the context of the Generative Proto-Architectures studio led by Michael Hensel and myself at Rice School of Architecture. This experiment was driven by the hypothesis that the material capacity of a system consisting of uniform elements can be employed to achieve variable yet stable configurations with complex curvature through a vast array of local actuations.

Initial tests confirmed that a series of very simple rectangular wooden elements fastened to a larger sheet of timber can be deployed as local actuators. Each rectangular element is attached to a larger patch by four bolts, one in each corner. While two of the bolts in opposite corners are permanently fixed and thereby define the length of the diagonal line between them, the other two bolts remain adjustable. Tightening these two bolts increases the distance between the element's corners and the patch begins to bend. As each larger patch is covered with arrays of elements, the incremental induction of curvature results in a global (de)formation. Detailed investigations of the correlation of element and patch variables such as size, thickness and fibre orientation, actuator locations and torque lead to taxonomy of geometric patterns and generated system behaviour. This data enabled scripting of the parametric definition, assembly sequence and actuation protocols for a large prototype construction.

The configuration tested as a large-scale prototype consists of initially flat, identical timber patches onto which equal elements with actuator bolts are attached on one side. According to the particular distribution of actuator positions, the elements are connected to the patches and the patches are assembled into a larger structure with different orientations of the element's clad sides. The resulting material system consists of 48 identical patches, 1920 equal elements and 7680 bolts. After assembly, the structure is initially entirely flat. Through the subsequent incremental actuation of fastening

Differential surface actuation
Top to bottom: Close-up view of actuation elements and patches (left) and resulting light transmission patterns (right); Metapatch prototype at the 'Modulations' exhibition, Rice School of Architecture, Houston, US, November 2004; parametric definition and actuation protocol for full-scale prototype.

delineated bolts it then rises into a stable, self-supporting state with alternating convex and concave curvature. Changes to variables within this actuation protocol allow for articulating and testing multiple emergent states and their inherent performative capacity. As the patches are perforated by drilled hole-patterns, the performative modulation of porosity and the adjustment of structural capacity through curvature are intrinsically correlated with the manipulation of the system's material and geometric behaviour. Developing an integral technique of form generating and making based on the material capacity and local actuation of the system enabled a variable, complex morphology derived through the materiality, geometry and interaction of amazingly simple material elements.

Component Differentiation and Proliferation: Paper-Strip Experiment

A third approach towards polymorphous material systems is component differentiation and proliferation. While the experiment explained above relied on the differential actuation of equal components, the following morphogenetic technique is based on parametric components defined through geometric relationships. The proliferation of different instantiations of a parametric component generates a material system with differentiated sublocations. I developed such a design process through an experiment[7] based on very simple material components, namely twisted and bent paper-strips.

In this project, a digital component is defined as an open and extendable geometric framework based on the 'logics' of a material system that integrates the possibilities and limits of making, and the self-forming tendencies and constraints of the material. Through elaborate physical studies of the behaviour of twisted and bent paper-strips, the essential geometric features, such as points of curvature, developability of the surface and tangency alignments were captured in a digital component. This component describes the nonmetric geometric associations of a single paper-strip as part of a component collective and thereby anticipates the process of assembly and integration into a larger system. In other words, through parametric geometric relationships the digital component ensures that any morphology generated can be materialised as strips cut from sheet material.

A larger system can then be established through a process of proliferating components into polymorphic populations. For this, a variable 'proliferation environment' is defined to provide the constraints for the accretion of components as well as stimuli/inputs for their individual morphologies. An algorithm drives the distribution of components with three possible modes of proliferation: first, an outward proliferation of a component into a population that increases in number until the environment's boundaries are reached, second, an inward proliferation within the initial system's setup and, third, a hierarchical proliferation based on environments/inputs for secondary, tertiary, etc, systems. These three proliferation

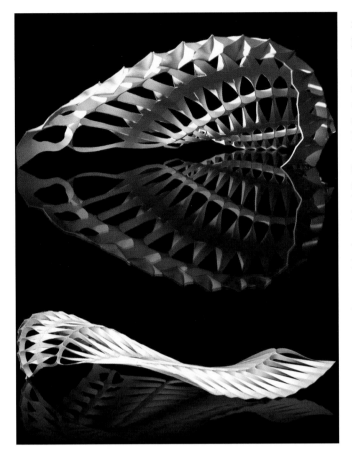

Component differentiation and proliferation
Physical test models of paper-strip system derived through a parametric process embedding the material characteristics, manufacturing constraints and assembly logics observed in physical tests.

modes can also be deployed in combination, leading to nested populations of component systems.

The resulting system remains open to 'local' manipulation of individual components, 'regional' manipulation of component collectives and 'global' manipulations of the component system, proliferation environment and distribution algorithm. The parametric associations of and between components, collectives and the overall system allow the rapid implementation of these manipulations, leading to a multitude of self-updating system instances. Situated in a simulated environment of external forces, the system's behavioural tendencies then reveal its performative capacity. For example, exposing multiple system instances to digitally simulated light flow enables the registration of interrelations between parametric manipulations and the modulation of light levels upon and beyond the system.

Additional digital structural analyses of the same instances reveal the related load-bearing behaviour of the system. These behavioural tendencies of the system interacting with external forces and modulating transmitted flows can be traced across various parametrically defined individual morphologies. The resulting patterns of force distribution and conditions of varying luminous intensity can inform further cycles of local, regional and global parametric manipulations. Continually informing the open parametric framework of component definition and proliferation yields an increasing differentiation with the capacity for negotiating multiple-performance criteria within one system. The important point is that the outlined parametric design technique permits the

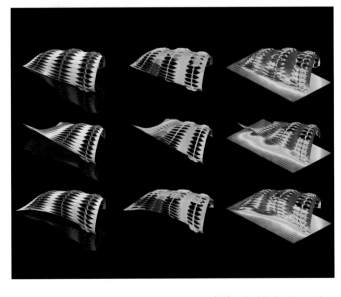

Geometric manipulations of the parametric system (left) and related patterns of structural behaviour (centre: contour plots of finite element analysis under gravity load) and modulation of light conditions (right: geographically specific illuminance analysis on the system and a register surface for an overcast sky).

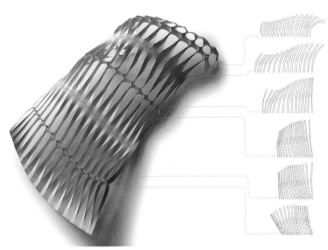

Physical test model of a population of 90 paper-strip components and related strip-cut patterns

recognition of patterns of geometric behaviour and related performative capacities of the polymorphous component population. In continued feedback with the external environment, these behavioural tendencies can then inform the ontogenetic development of a specific system through the parametric differentiation of its sublocations. And these processes of differentiation will always remain consistent with the constraints of materialisation, fabrication and assembly of the paper-strips.

Generative Algorithmic Definition: Honeycomb Morphologies

Another technique for the development of a polymorphous cellular structure has been researched by Andrew Kudless for his Masters dissertation[8] as part of the AA Emergent Technologies and Design programme led by Michael

Weinstock, Michael Hensel and myself. While in the paper-strip experiment the material, manufacturing and assembly logics were embedded in a digital component corresponding to the physical element to be proliferated into a larger population, the focus in this project is to algorithmically generate a coherent honeycomb system able to colonise variable geometric envelopes within the limits of fabrication.

Standard honeycomb systems are limited to planar or regularly curved geometry due to their equal cell sizes resulting from the constraints of industrial mass-production. However, computer-aided manufacturing (CAM) processes allow for a greatly increased range of geometries if the production logics become an integral part of the form-generation process. In this particular case, the embedding of manufacturing constraints in the rules of deriving the system required the consideration of three aspects for the construction of a large-

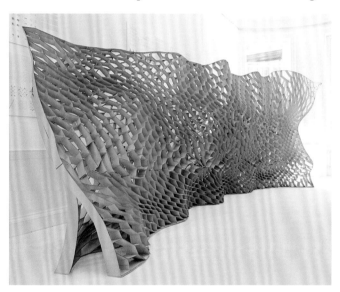

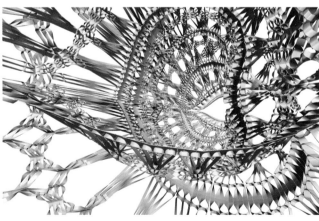

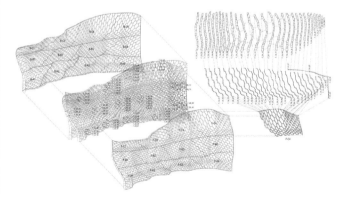

Component differentiation and proliferation
Parametric outward proliferation (top) and inward proliferation of the system (bottom).

Generative algorithmic definition
Differentiated honeycomb morphology prototype exhibited at the AA Projects Review, July 2004 (top), and digital model of differentiated honeycomb morphology (bottom left) from which the manufacturing data is extracted (bottom right).

scale prototype. First, to ensure topological continuity all generated cells need to remain hexagonal and tangential with the adjacent cell walls. Second, folded material strips of which the system consists are cut from planar sheet material with a laser, therefore the possible generation of elements must be linked to the constraints of the related production technique, namely two-dimensional cutting of limited size and the specific material properties such as, for example, the folding behaviour. The third important point is the anticipation of required assembly logistics through labelling all elements and inherently defining the construction sequence by the uniqueness of each pair of matching cell walls.

Based on these aspects, the resultant digital generation process comprises the following sequence. In order to define the eventual vertices of the honeycomb strips, points are digitally mapped across a surface that is defined by the

Generative algorithmic definition
Algorithmically derived honeycomb prototype in which each cell is unique in shape, size and depth, allowing for changing cell densities and double-curved global geometry (top), and close-up views showing planar connection tabs between honeycomb layers (bottom left) and double-curved global surface articulation (bottom right).

designer and remains open to geometric manipulations. The parametrically defined correlation of point distribution and geometric surface characteristics can also be altered. An algorithmic procedure that connects the distributed points creates the required folded strip lines. Looping this algorithm across all points forms the honeycomb mesh, and this procedure is repeated across an offset point distribution to generate a system wire-frame model. In a following step the defined honeycomb strips are unfolded, labelled and nested to prepare for subsequent production.

This integral form-generation and fabrication process can create honeycomb systems in which each cell can be unique in shape, size and depth, allowing for changing cell densities and a large range of irregularly curved global geometries. The resultant differentiation in the honeycomb has considerable performance consequences, as the system now carries the capacity for adaptation to specific structural, environmental and other forces not only within the overall system, but locally across different sublocations of varying cell size, depth and orientation. Embedding the possibilities and constraints of material and production technology, the form-generation technique and its parametric definition become, per se, the main interface of negotiating multiple-performance criteria.

Digital Growth and Ontogenetic Drifts: Fibrous Surfaces
The final project synthesises the presented methods of component differentiation and mapped propagation with digitally simulated growth.[9] This collaborative project,[10] developed by Sylvia Felipe, Jordi Truco and myself together with Emmanuel Rufo and Udo Thoennissen, aims to evolve a differentiated surface structure consisting of a dense network of interlocking members from a basic array of simple, straight elements. To achieve complexity in the resultant material system the exploration focuses on advanced digital generation techniques in concert with relatively common computer numerically controlled (CNC) production processes.

The basic system constituent is defined as a jagged, planar strip cut from sheet material on a three-axis CNC router. In a parametric software application a generic digital component is established through the geometric relationships that remain invariant in all possible instances of the material element and the variable production constraints of the intended machining technology and process. Each particular implementation of the parametric component in the system to be digitally constructed is then based on three interrelated inputs. Primary input influencing the particular geometry of a specific system type is given by a Gestalt envelope that describes the system's overall extent and shape. This envelope is defined by a geometric surface grown in a digitally simulated environment of forces. The digital growth process employed for the generation of the surface is based on extended Lindenmayer systems (L-systems), which produce form through the interaction of two factors: a geometric seed combined with rewriting rules that specify how elements of the shape change, and a process that repeatedly reinterprets the rules with respect to the current shape.

In this particular case the surface is represented by a graph data structure constituted by a set of edges, vertices and regions. Since all edges are constantly rewritten during the digital growth process, all parts of the surface continuously change until the ontogenetic drifts[11] settle into a stable configuration. Based on the growing surface, another input for the implementation of the material elements is generated. In response to particular geometric surface features such as global undulation and regional curvature, a variable distribution algorithm establishes a network of lines on the surface indicating the position of each element and the related node type. Digital components then populate the system accordingly and construct a virtual solid model. In the resultant organisation, crossing members only intersect if they are perpendicular due to the embedded manufacturing constraints. If not, they pass under or over crossing elements, not dissimilar to a bird's nest, and thereby form a geometrically defined, self-interlocking, stable structure.

This complex correlation of geometric definition, structural behaviour and production logics does not only remain coherent in a single system, such as the tested prototype with almost 90 members and 1000 joints, but is integral to the generation process itself. This is of particular importance if one considers that the surface defining the critical morphogenetic input is constructed through a bottom-up process in which all parts respond to local interactions and the environment. As these internal and external interactions are complex and the interpretation of the L-systems is nonlinear, the outcome of the growth process remains open-ended. This continual change, combined with the long-chain dependencies of the subsequent generation methods, enables the growth of different system types of member organisation, system topology and consequent performative capacity. Such an integral design approach begins to expand the notion of performative polymorphic systems towards digital typogenesis.

While the five experiments presented here remain in a proto-architectural state awaiting implementation in a specific architectural context, the related morphogenetic design techniques and technologies allow for the rethinking of the nature of currently established design processes. A design approach utilising such methods enables architects to define specific material systems through the combined logics of formation and materialisation. It promotes replacing the creation of specific shapes subsequently rationalised for realisation and superimposed functions, through the unfolding of performative capacities inherent to the material arrangements and constructs we derive. Most importantly, it encourages the fundamental rethinking of our current mechanical approaches to sustainability and a related functionalist understanding of efficiency. ∆

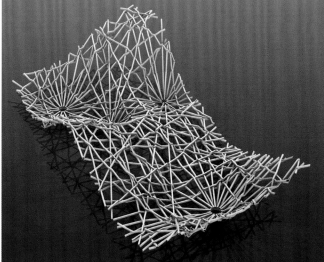

Digital growth and ontogenetic drifts
Diagram: The surface geometry generated through a digital growth process based on extended Lindenmayer systems (bottom) provides the geometric data for an algorithmic distribution of parametric components (centre), which results in a complex network of self-interlocking straight members (top) that are immediately ready for production.
Above: View of fibrous self-interlocking surface structure.

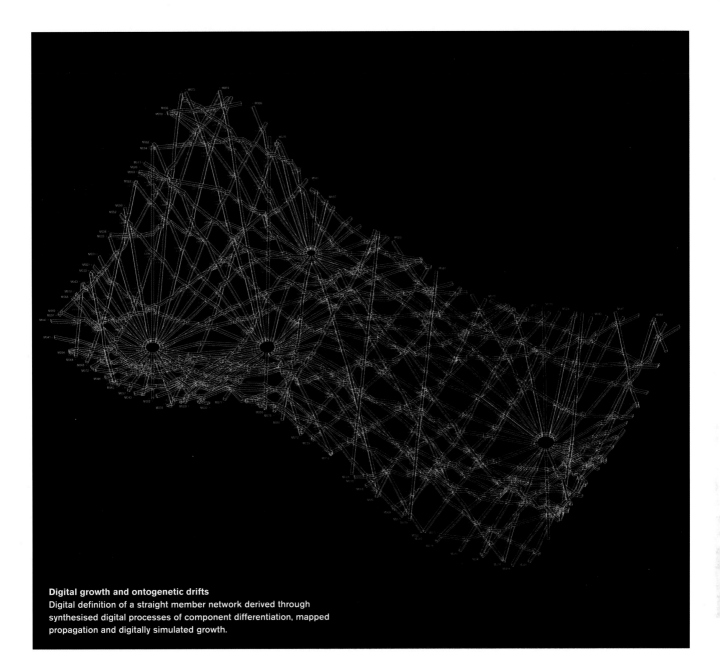

Digital growth and ontogenetic drifts
Digital definition of a straight member network derived through
synthesised digital processes of component differentiation, mapped
propagation and digitally simulated growth.

Notes
1. Homologous systems share an
evolutionary transformation from the
same 'ancestral' state.
2. Polytypic species are species that
comprise several subspecies or
variants.
3. The organisational potentialities of
complex built environments have been
outlined in Achim Menges, 'Morpho-
ecologies: approaching complex
environments, *D Emergence:
Morphogenetic Design Strategies*, pp
48–53, Vol 74, No 3, 2004.
4. 'Membrane Morphologies'
Morphogenetic Design Experiment
04, April 2004 to Sept 2005. Phase
01: Physical and Digital Form-
Finding Developments (Michael
Hensel and Achim Menges, with
Giorgos Kailis and Nikolaos
Stathopoulos). Phase 02: Exhibition

installation at the AA School of
Architecture, London, 2004 (Michael
Hensel and Achim Menges, with
Tiffany Beriro, Edouard Cabay and
Valeria Segovia). Phase 03:
Exhibition installation at Rice School
of Architecture, Houston, 2004
(Michael Hensel and Achim Menges).
5. See 'Frei Otto in Conversation with
the Emergent and Design Group', *D
Emergence: Morphogenetic Design
Strategies*, pp. 19–25.
6. Joseph Kellner and David Newton,
'Metapatch' project, Generative
Proto-Architectures Studio, Rice
School of Architecture, Houston,
September to December 2004.
Visiting professors: Michael Hensel
and Achim Menges. Visiting staff:
Neri Oxman and Andrew Kudless.
7. 'Paper-Strip Morphologies'
Morphogenetic Design Experiment

03, April 2004 to April 2005. Phase
01: Physical and Digital Form-
Finding Developments (Achim
Menges with Andrew Kudless,
Ranidia Leeman and Michuan Xu).
Phase 02: Parametric Set-Up and
Proliferation (Achim Menges); Finite
Element Analysis (Nikolaos
Stathopoulos).
8. Andrew Kudless, 'Manifold –
Honeycomb Morphologies' MA
dissertation project, Emergent
Technologies and Design Masters
programme, AA Graduate School of
Architecture, London, 2004.
Programme directors: Michael
Hensel and Michael Weinstock.
Studio master: Achim Menges.
9. See Dr Una-May O'Reilly, Martin
Hemberg and Achim Menges,
'Evolutionary Computation and
Artificial Life in Architecture', *D

Emergence: Morphogenetic Design
Strategies*, pp. 48–53.
10. 'Fibrous Surfaces'
Morphogenetic Design Experiment
05, June 2004 to October 2005.
Phase 01: 'Integral Envelopes'
Workshop (Sylvia Felipe, Achim
Menges, Jordi Truco, Emmanuel Rufo
and Udo Thoennissen), ESARQ
International University of Catalunya,
Barcelona. Phase 02: Algorithmic
Distribution and Material Tests
(Emmanuel Rufo, Sylvia Felipe,
Achim Menges, Udo Thoennissen
and Jordi Truco). Phase 03: Material
Prototype (Emmanuel Rufo, Sylvia
Felipe, Achim Menges and Jordi
Truco).
11. Ontogenetic drifts are the
developmental changes in form and
function that are inseparable from
growth.

Material and Digital Design Synthesis

Integrating material self-organisation, digital morphogenesis, associative parametric modelling and computer-aided manufacturing

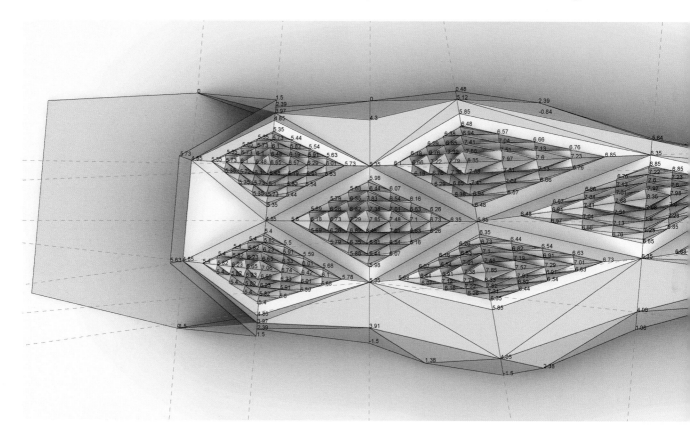

The advanced material and morphogenetic digital design techniques and technologies presented in this journal call for a higher level methodological integration, which poses a major challenge for the next generation of multidisciplinary architectural research and projects. This collaborative task encompasses the striving for an integrated set of design methods, generative and analytical tools and enabling technologies that facilitate and instrumentalise evolutionary design, and evaluation of differentiated material systems towards a highly performative and sustainable built environment. **Michael Hensel** and **Achim Menges** describe recent progress towards a higher-level design synthesis of material self-organisation, digital morphogenesis, associative parametric modelling and computer-aided manufacturing (CAM) on the basis of two works produced within the context of the Emergent Technologies and Design Masters programme at the Architectural Association in London, and a recent competition entry by Scheffler + Partner Architects and Achim Menges.

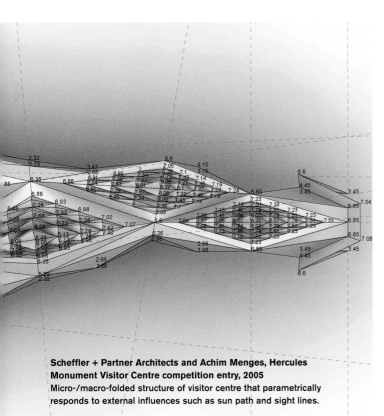

Scheffler + Partner Architects and Achim Menges, Hercules Monument Visitor Centre competition entry, 2005
Micro-/macro-folded structure of visitor centre that parametrically responds to external influences such as sun path and sight lines.

Imagine, thirdly, that the digital components that are geometrically characterised by material behaviour and materialisation processes populate evolving geometric host environments, such as surfaces or branch-like geometric structures, to form larger assemblies. Imagine that these base geometries are evolved by means of growth or evolutionary algorithms, so that many individuals and various generations of the system can be evolved in response to the increasing level of articulation of the input geometry.

Then imagine that the growth or evolution of component assemblies can be informed on various scales of the system by multiple extrinsic influences, such as exposure to sunlight, prevailing wind directions, and so on. Negotiating between different and probably conflicting system-intrinsic criteria like manufacturing and construction constraints embedded in the underlying parametric setup, and multiple environmental influences, the system would unfold levels of increasingly complex articulation that could be ranked according to their ability to satisfy multiple goals and performance objectives. In exchange with appropriate analysis and evaluation techniques, this could even lead to a co-evolution of the driving criteria enabling an integral yet environmentally sensitive design process.

The following projects have focused on different aspects of such a higher-level material and digital design integration, yet seen together they provide insights into a latent synthesis of various techniques and technologies in morphogenetic design that have all, individually, already begun to alter current perceptions and practice of architecture.

Giannis Douridas and Mattia Gambardella, AA Emergent Technologies and Design, Associative Component Structures, 2005

The research by Giannis Douridas and Mattia Gambardella, an AA EmTech team, aimed at setting up a geometric scaffold in an associative parametric modelling environment that consists of a subdivided host surface defined through two perimeter curves. The curves themselves are each defined by sets of three points, of which each central point's coordinates are iteratively altered by a function driven through a coefficient that calls pseudo-random numbers. Within a range defined through maximum and minimum allowed values, each numerical value generated results in a host geometry that provides the relevant U and V surface domain and normal vectors for the insertion of parametric components.

Within the specific UVN parameter space of each macro-geometric surface, two component types are to be populated. First, an array of local coordinate systems provides the surface normal vectors at variable intervals. At the same parameter coordinate position the curvature of the surface is analysed and, through a defined function, provides a specific offset distance for a rib structure of iso-parametric curves. As the curvature changes across all generated surface instances

Today, a paradigm shift can emerge from multiple discrete innovations that when brought together achieve a significant shift in operativity and design production. In this issue of $\triangle$, numerous morphogenetic design methods, techniques and technologies have been introduced, but eventually the question arises as to what all this amounts to, and what would happen if these processes were synthesised into a coherent toolset.

Imagine, firstly, digital associative parametric modelling that is informed by physical form-finding experiments, with self-organisational characteristics of materials and material systems rigorously encoded in a series of geometric relations and dependencies, so that these characteristics are retained across all system instances resulting from changes to parametric variables of the digital model.

Imagine, secondly, that the geometric relations and dependencies that characterise the setup and constituents of the associative digital model are, in addition, informed by computer-aided manufacturing (CAM) constraints of the material components so that each digitally defined system can be directly manufactured and assembled.

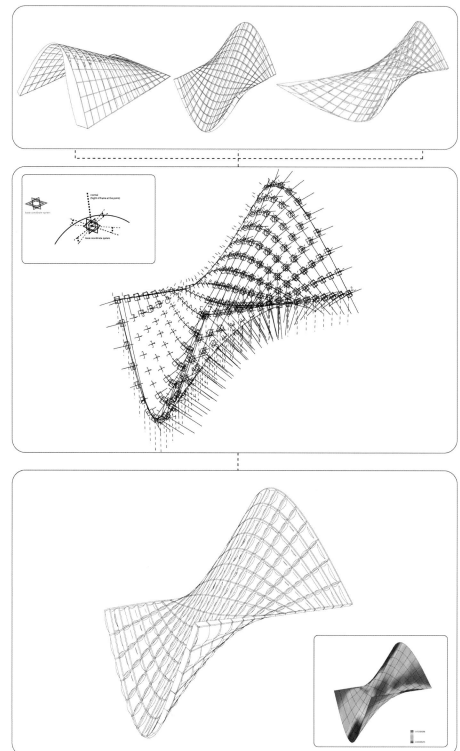

Giannis Douridas and Mattia Gambardella, Associative Componenent Structures, 2005
Three surface instances of a parametrically defined geometric scaffold responding to pseudo-random numeric input (top); one surface populated with local coordinate systems in response to its specific UVN parameter space (middle); three different component types populating the local coordinate system array on the surface (bottom).

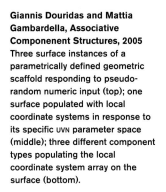

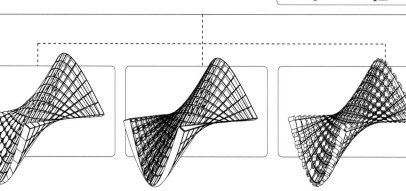

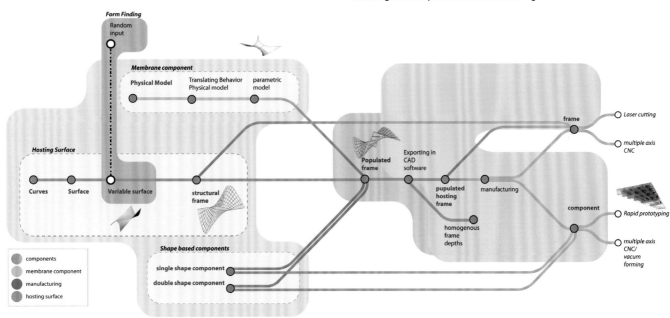

Giannis Douridas and Mattia Gambardella, Associative Component Structures, 2005
Flow chart of project investigations indicating operative interrelations of a synthesis of form generation, parametric modelling and computer-aided manufacturing.

and along each individual surface, the depth and orientation of the ribs changes accordingly. The second digital component reads the polygonal shape and its geometric features, such as edge length, angle, and so on, which is given through four local coordinate systems as input data. As various component types are capable of processing this input and adapting accordingly, the team chose a series of components defined by themselves, or by other EmTech and Diploma Unit 4 teams, to test and develop their scaffold. A variety of synclastic and anticlastic surface curvatures were evolved and tested.

Since all tested components are informed by manufacturing and construction constraints, each specific component assembly within the evolving geometric scaffold can be manufactured immediately, although the question of tolerances relative to each specific component still needs to be addressed. In the following step, the pseudo-random numbers that generate the curves, which in turn generate the host surfaces providing the specific geometric data for each component-type instance, can be related to extrinsic influences: for example, the local surface vectors of each individual component of a larger population can be defined in relation to the sun path, and so on. In doing so it becomes possible to inform, for instance, the overall or regional articulation of a building envelope and to embed multiple-performance capacity in the system.

Pavel Hladík, AA Emergent Technologies and Design, Phyllotaxic Component Growth, 2005

A second EmTech research project, by Pavel Hladík, aimed at implementing a growth algorithm and, more specifically, a Lindenmayer system (L-system) in an associative parametric modelling environment. The research commenced from form-finding experiments with an elastic net that wraps spherical solids fixed in a space, and was subsequently described as a series of geometric relations and dependencies that allowed the setting up of a generic parametric model. In a later step, a growth algorithm was implemented in the parametric modelling environment that enables the iterative rewriting of the underlying parametric definition. The application of L-systems provides the necessary rewriting and production rules for a digital growth process of a parametric component. The primary growth steps are parametrically defined through spherical and cylindrical coordinate systems. The secondary articulation follows a phyllotactic pattern and related mathematical models of plant growth. In botany, phyllotaxis describes the arrangement of the leaves, buds, thorns and so on of the plant. The regular arrangement of plant organs forms spirals or parastichies and can be alternate, opposite, whorled or in a spiral.

In this research project, smaller system constituents are proliferated in the defined parameter space and provide potential subcomponent interfaces at situations where growing macro-components begin to intersect. Furthermore, the growth of the macro-components and the propagation of micro-components within the growing host geometries can be related to extrinsic influences, as is the case with phyllotaxis, by which plant elements are packed and/or oriented towards environmental influences. The parastichies inform the geometric definition of a scaffold made from laser-cut sheet material on which tubular rods can be formed and welded together and subcomponents can be attached to the helical body. In this way, it is possible to grow and construct a material system that can be informed by tropism, the turning or bending movement of an organism or a part towards or away from an external stimulus, such as light, heat or gravity,

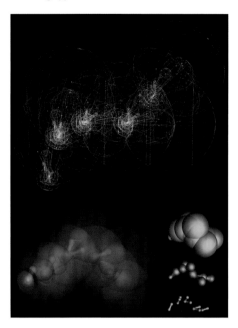

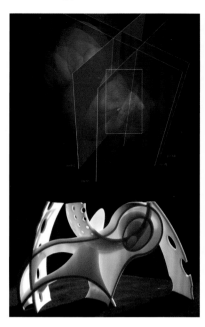

and an optimised disposition of elements and subcomponents, for example photovoltaic panels, that are directly informed by the macro-articulation of the system due to tropism.

Scheffler + Partner Architects and Achim Menges, Hercules Monument Visitor Centre competition entry, 2005

While the two Emtech research projects focus on exploring and assessing a higher level of material and design synthesis through a primarily bottom-up design methodology, the following project investigates ways of instrumentalising integral form-generation techniques for a competition project for a historical site. In 2005, Achim Menges and Scheffler + Partner Architects (Professor Ernst Ulrich Scheffler and Eva Scheffler), in collaboration with Professor Dr Klaus Bollinger (Bollinger + Grohmann Consulting Engineers) and Claudius Grothe (Freiraum Landscape Architecture) developed a competition design for a visitor centre for the Hercules monument in Bergpark Wilhelmshöhe, Germany, which is on the list of prospective world heritage sites. Situated at the 515-metre (1690-foot) high peak of a major Baroque sight axis of Kassel Wilhelmshöhe Palace and a 250-metre (820-foot) long water cascade, the 71 metres (233 feet) tall Hercules monument was designed by Francesco Guerniero and completed in 1717.

Due to the complex historical situation, the proposal for the visitor centre suggests an infolding of the park to articulate an interior landscape submerged underground that intensifies the transition from the natural surrounding of Habichtswald to the Baroque park and monument. Thus, rather than relating the competition brief to specific spatial entities that aim at directly answering the programmatic and volumetric requirements, the project's spatial strategy is based on providing an interior environment made up of different micro-milieus. These offer a range of luminous conditions, surface articulations and views

along each visitor's path to the Hercules monument through strategic penetrations of the exterior park by which the structure is covered. Thus the western approach to Wilhelmshöhe through the visitor centre is articulated as a series of terrains that allow each visitor to choose individual itineraries and sojourns as a personal response to daily and seasonal changes of light intensities, different vistas, programmatic provisions and duration of visit. By means of synthesising digital form-generation and associative modelling techniques, a system of self-similar triangulated faces across multiple scales of articulation and performativity became instrumental in the development of the design proposal.

The biomimetic principle of self-similarity underlies the setup of a parametrically defined and constrained triangulated system with four interdependent scales of articulation: central to the performative strategy are arrays of triangular micro-folds nested on the faces of quadrilateral pyramids which themselves are parts of the macro-folds that articulate the overall geometry of the system. Each scale of resolution shares the basic parametric setup defined through triangular geometry, but responds to different input parameters in the iterative development process of the system. These underlying geometric associations are informed by the constraints of manufacturing and construction, ranging from computer numerically controlled (CNC) cut planar formwork for the in-situ concrete of the triangulated structural main body, to the folded-glass and steel plates of the micro-tessellation. The strategic negotiation of geometric control parameters of independent and interdependent system constituents enables an increasing level of complexity through nonlinear responses to the system-intrinsic constraints, performative criteria and surrounding environment during the generation of system variants. This synthesis of generative digital design tools and

Scheffler + Partner Architects and Achim Menges, Hercules Monument Visitor Centre competition entry, 2005
Axonometric view of sectional model showing the articulation of macro-, medium- and micro-triangulation derived through the response of the parametrically defined system to various performative criteria.

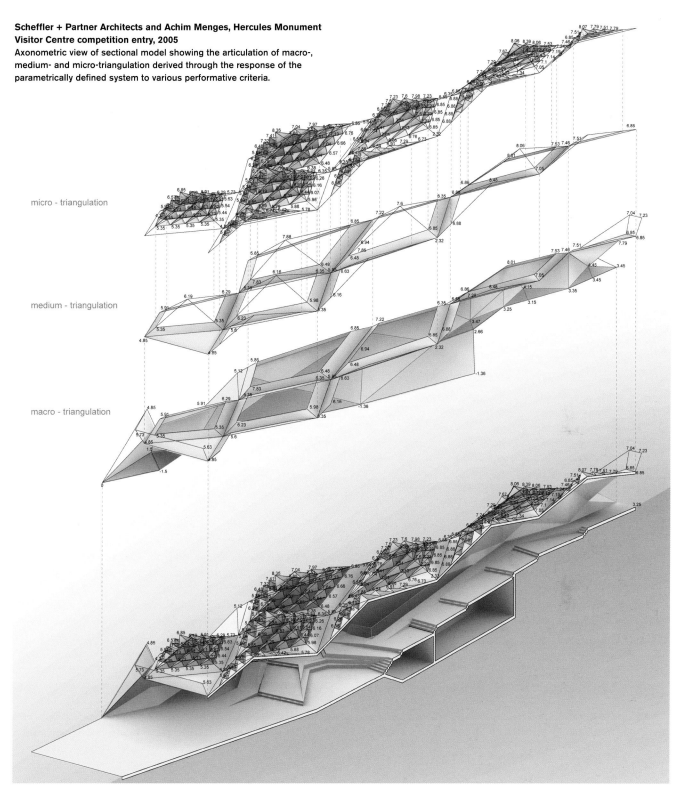

micro - triangulation

medium - triangulation

macro - triangulation

long-chain parametric dependencies assures coherence with a series of defined criteria, while at the same time allowing for novel and undetermined performative capacities to emerge through the negotiation of a top-down and bottom-up approach.

The setup of such an operative interrelation of system constraints, definition and capacity to achieve a differentiated landscape, 'lightscape' and 'viewscape' is explained as follows. The Baroque central axis and sight line provides the notional spine of the parametric control rig of the visitor centre's

overall geometry, which adapts to the circulatory and volumetric requirements and coheres with the structural needs of an underground, tunnel-like building. As a response to the specific vertical and horizontal forces resulting from self-weight, earth thrust and live loads interacting with the overall geometry, the main body is further articulated through a series of macro-folds. For example, a framework of V-shaped trusses with sufficient structural depth carries the dead and live loads of the park and micro-fold articulations

Site plan (top) and section (bottom) of the historical Hercules monument and the proposed visitor centre.

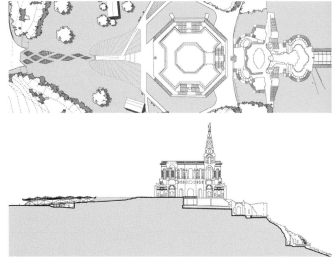

above, while the triangulated walls counteract the earth thrust and transfer the loads into the sole plate and medium-triangulation of the structure. The orientation and inclination of the faces of the medium-triangulation distributes the forces resulting from the glass-and-steel micro-triangulated system. The adaptation to the specific forces is constantly negotiated with the notional parametric constraint envelope of the interior landscape given, for example, through clear heights, surface inclinations, maximum slopes, areas and volumes. Furthermore, the orientation of the medium fold-lines, the related edge vectors and surface normals are set up in relation to the sun path and transmittance and reflection of light. At the same time they define the main fields of view and sight lines. These become further differentiated through the nested micro-triangulation of self-supporting folded glass and stainless-steel plates.

Within the main viewing fields organised by the medium fold-lines and dimensions, the micro-triangulation differentiates the vistas towards the Hercules monument and surrounding landscape. From different viewpoints within the interior landscape, the monument is exposed, framed, partially visible or entirely hidden. Along the individual path of each visitor, the views experienced change from obstructed, framed and open vistas that culminate in the direct exposure of the enormous monument when transiting from the infolded interior landscape to the Baroque park. In addition, the micro-folds' geometric differentiation of face sizes, heights and orientations also modulates the transmission and reflection of luminous flow during the daily and annual changes of the sun path. As a result, dynamic fields of differential light intensity and solar gain emerge in correlation with different fields of view, providing dynamic micro-environmental zones and programmatic opportunities. Not dissimilar to the partial transmittance of light through leaves in the adjacent forest, the micro-shades resulting from this articulation allow the inhabitants to choose from a wide range of luminous

Scheffler + Partner Architects and Achim Menges, Hercules Monument Visitor Centre competition entry, 2005
Plan (top) and sectional (bottom) articulation of the interior landscape, 'lightscape' and 'viewscape' of the proposed visitor centre.

Interior view of the visitor centre indicating the visitor's differentiated field of obstructed, framed and open views towards the Hercules monument.

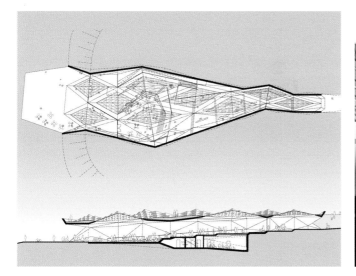

intensities in the café, lounge, waiting and information areas. At the same time, the high number of differently orientated faces reflects the light of the polished stainless-steel and glass surfaces to extend the Baroque concept of the adjacent water cascades through a cascade of reflected and refracted light.

The generative drivers and system-intrinsic and -extrinsic control parameters can be strategically altered in various design iterations within the editable and nonlinear design history of the project. Through this synthesis of form generation and associative parametric modelling, which embeds the geometric constraints of the related fabrication and construction processes, a greater degree of coherency and/or strategic incongruence can be achieved. This setup then yields complex, unpredictable and undetermined performative effects through which alternative spatial strategies can be implemented and explored. Although the digital setup, as well as the material/structural systems, is organised hierarchically, the integral nature of this design process enables each scale of definition to implicitly address a whole series of defined criteria and performative aspects. Through the continuous negotiation of these constraints and the resulting defined, anticipated and novel performative effects, the integral capacity of the system emerges. The investigation and evaluation of these emergent capacities then allows for the redefinition of the driving criteria, and thereby provides an inroad for a critical and innovative approach to architectural design.

Besides the work undertaken by Michael Hensel, Achim Menges, Michael Weinstock and Nikolaos Stathopoulos in the Emergence and Design Group and at the Architectural Association, there are a number of contexts in which related important work is currently being undertaken. Three related lines of research critical to a higher level of material and design integration are currently under way: 1) a rigorous and instrumental analysis of living nature leading to major advances in designing composite materials with higher functionality as pursued, for example, at the Centre for Biomimetic Engineering at the University of Reading led by Professor George Jeronimidis; 2) research into advanced adaptable structures and alternative approaches to environmentally modulating building envelopes, such as that conducted by Professor Werner Sobek and his team at the Institute for Lightweight Design and Construction (ILEK – the former IL Institute for Lightweight Structures of Frei Otto); 3) new ways of understanding and designing morphologies, as investigated by Professor Mark Burry at the technical office of the Temple Sagrada Família, RMIT University in Melbourne and UPC University of Catalunya. These lines of research promise very interesting results that can feed into a rigorous and instrumental higher-level methodological integration as described in this article, out of which a higher-level functionality and performance-oriented design paradigm might arise.

Overall, the argument and instrumental toolset that begins to emerge operates largely on gradient threshold conditions and effects and their experiential value. In the next stage of development, it would be interesting and necessary to re-engage a discourse of spatial arrangement and social formation that operates on the combination of the hard material thresholds and the environmental gradient threshold. Topological alterations of each evolved design instance may thus yield alternative and novel spatial arrangements together with the social formation pattern that these spaces can provide for. On the whole, the possibility for this renewed discourse is perhaps the most significant indicator of a paradigm shift in architectural design and a relevant topic for a future issue of ⟁. ⟁

Project credits
Hercules Monument Visitor Centre competition entry, 2005
Architects: Scheffler + Partner Architects (Professor Ernst Ulrich Scheffler and Eva Scheffler) in collaboration with Professor Achim Menges.
Structural engineers: Bollinger + Grohmann Consulting Engineers (Professor Klaus Bollinger and Mark Fahlbusch).
Landscape Architect: Freiraum (Claudius Grothe).

Contributors

Michael U Hensel is an architect, urban designer, researcher and writer. He is a partner in OCEAN NORTH and the Emergence and Design Group, as well as a board member of the BIONIS (Biomimetics Network for Industrial Sustainability) management committee. He has held visiting professorships, taught, lectured, exhibited and published in Europe, the Americas, and the Middle and Far East, and teaches at the AA, where he is director of the Emergent Technologies and Design Masters programme and unit master of Diploma Unit 4. In 2004 he received the tutor prize of the Royal Institute of Architects. His research interests include a synthetic life approach to architecture, a biological paradigm for architectural design and sustainability of the built environment, based on differentiated and multiple-performative material systems, spatial arrangements and social formations, as well as contributing to a critical discourse on politics of space. Forthcoming publications include, with Achim Menges, *Morpho-Ecologies* (AA Publications, 2006). www.politicsofspace.net, www.ocean-north.net, www.emergence-and-design.org, www.aaschool.ac.uk/et, www.extra.rdg.ac.uk/eng/BIONIS

Professor Achim Menges is an architect and partner in OCEAN NORTH and the Emergence and Design Group. He studied at the Technical University Darmstadt and graduated from the AA with Honours. He has taught at the AA since 2002 and is currently unit master of Diploma Unit 4 and studio master of the Emergent Technologies and Design Masters programme. He has also been a visiting professor at Rice University School of Architecture, Houston. Since 2005 he has been Professor for Form Generation and Materialization at the HfG Offenbach University for Art and Design in Germany. His research focuses on the development of integral design processes at the intersection of evolutionary computation, parametric design, biomimetic engineering and computer-aided manufacturing that enable a highly articulated, performative built environment. His research projects have been published and exhibited in Europe, Asia and the US. He received the

FEIDAD (Far Eastern International Digital Architectural Design) Outstanding Design Award in 2002, the FEIDAD Design Merit Award in 2003, the Archiprix International Award 2003, RIBA Tutor Price 2004 and the International Bentley Educator of the Year Award 2005. www.achimmenges.net, www.ocean-north.net, www.emergence-and-design.org, www.aaschool.ac.uk/et

Nikolaos Stathopoulos studied engineering and computational mechanics at the University of Patras, Greece, and also studied emergent technologies and design at the AA, where he is now a tutor of technical studies. He is a structural engineer at Whitbybird Engineers, London, and has recently lectured at Yale School of Architecture. His research and teaching at the AA focus on the simulation of complex structural systems – including natural material systems – and the nonlinear processes and dynamics involved.

Michael Weinstock is an architect. Born in Germany, he lived as a child in the Far East and then West Africa, and attended an English public school. He ran away to sea at the age of 17 after reading Conrad. After many years at sea, in traditional sailing ships where he gained shipyard and shipbuilding experience, he studied architecture at the AA and has taught at the AA School of Architecture since 1989 as unit master and master of technical studies. He is a co-founder and co-director, with Michael Hensel, of the AA Emergent Technologies and Design Masters programme. He is currently lecturing on evolutionary design at Yale School of Architecture and is also a visiting professor to the postgraduate research programme Genetic Architectures, at ESARQ, Barcelona. His research interests lie in exploring the convergence of biomimetic engineering, emergence and material sciences, and he has published widely on these topics. The potential of convergence for the materialisation of intelligent materials, structures, buildings and, ultimately, the organisation of cities, provides the motivation and suggests the long-term goal. www.emergence-and-design.org, www.aaschool.ac.uk/et

The Emergence and Design Group was formed in 2002 as a multidisciplinary design and research practice based in London. The group undertakes design and research that combines architecture, industrial design, biomimetic engineering, digital morphogenesis, as well as advanced CAD/CAE/CAM, and explores design approaches based on evolutionary design, self-organisation and emergence. Michael Hensel, Achim Menges, Nikolaos Stathopoulos and Michael Weinstock lead the group, which collaborates extensively with Buro Happold in London, and Professor George Jeronimidis and the Centre of Biomimetic Engineering at the University of Reading. The group has also started the Emergence and Design Network which brings together eminent experts and researchers in the disciplines that are related to the group's extensive research activities. Recent publications include ⚙ *Emergence: Morphogenetic Design Strategies*, Vol 74, No 3, 2004. www.emergence-and-design.org

OCEAN NORTH is an experimental and multidisciplinary design collective that undertakes design research, projects and consultancy in the intersection between urban design, architecture, industrial design and cultural production. Michael Hensel, Achim Menges and Birger Sevaldson organise the think tank. OCEAN NORTH's work has been widely published and exhibited in Europe, Asia and the Americas. Recent projects include the World Center for Human Affairs, exhibited at 'A New World Trade Center' at the Max Protetch Gallery in New York, the Venice Architectural Biennale in 2002 and the 'Blobjects' exhibition at San Jose Museum of Art in 2005, as well as the Jyväskylä Music and Art Center, exhibited at the Venice Architectural Biennale in 2004. ⚙

Contents

98+

106+

Plus, Plus Ça Change at the Museum of Modern Art in New York

The selection of Yoshio Taniguchi, in 1997, to design the Museum of Modern Art's enormous expansion was generally considered conservative, if not outright old-fashioned. When the museum reopened in November 2004, most critics described the new scheme as 'contextual' or 'subtle', and noted that the architect had said he had tried 'to make the architecture go away'. Now that enough time has passed to blur expectations, Jayne Merkel looks at MoMA as it is today. She contends that the choice was progressive in exactly the way the museum has been all along, and that the architecture is very much there.

The new entrance to MoMA from West 53rd Street, looking east. A new book shop, designed by New York architect Richard Gluckman, is in the foreground. The Museum Tower apartment block, designed by Cesar Pelli in 1977, is in the background and is now an integral part of the composition.

No stone was left unturned before MoMA officials developed a programme and selected an architect for its $425 million, 23,410-square-metre (252,000-square-foot) expansion. They interviewed prominent artists, architects and critics exhaustively. Director Glenn Lowry and architectural curator Terence Riley, along with several department heads, lectured on the institution's history and aspirations to help prepare the public, trustees, staff and themselves for the work ahead. The building committee visited museums all over the world. A short list of contenders was then invited to submit little boxes filled with their

ideas. Finally, three finalists were asked to develop schemes in drawing and model form.

There were surprises all along the way. Although commissions for the museum's first three additions (in 1951, 1953 and 1964) had gone to its first curator of architecture, Philip Johnson, and the fourth had been awarded to the very experienced and nearby dean of the Yale School of Architecture, Cesar Pelli, none of the obvious candidates for the job were on the short list this time – not even Richard Meier, the home-town favourite who was just finishing the Getty Center and whose cool, white, geometric work

could have blended into the existing fabric. Neither was Frank Gehry, whose Bilbao Guggenheim was under construction and beginning to get raves. Only two of the other veterans of MoMA's own career-making 'Deconstructivist Architecture' show were included: Rem Koolhaas and Bernard Tschumi were on the short list with other members of what was considered the next generation (after Meier and Gehry). These were architects in their 50s (Taniguchi was actually the oldest): Wiel Arets, Jacques Herzog and Pierre de Meuron, Steven Holl, Toyo Ito, Koolhaas, Dominique Perrault, Tschumi, Rafael Viñoly and Tod Williams Billie Tsien and Associates.

The finalists were those who had presented the sparest, most pared-down entries. But both Tschumi and Herzog & de Meuron jazzed up their schemes in the second round, while Taniguchi simply restudied the problem, worked out the puzzle, polished his design very carefully – and got the job.

When the building opened seven years later, *New York Times* architecture critic Nicholas Ouroussoff, echoing the sentiments of many others, called it 'comforting', but said it 'may disappoint those who believe the museum's role should be as much about propelling the culture forward as about preserving our collective memory' (*New York Times*, 15 November 2004, E-1).

The building is a fine, beautifully detailed, almost invisible frame like the ones on the paintings it houses. But it is far more than that, for the problem of knitting together four previous building programmes (Johnson's first addition had been destroyed earlier), while expanding the building substantially and creating new circulation patterns and facilities without substantially changing the character of the whole, was no small task.

Taniguchi's redesign of the Museum of Modern Art emphatically locates the museum in the city. Views of surrounding buildings appear on gallery walls, like works in the collection. Even from the garden, the transparent new galleries appear part of the cityscape.

The Modern restaurant occupies a privileged position, accessible from its own entrance and lining the south side of the beloved walled garden that Philip Johnson created in 1953. Bentel & Bentel of New York designed all the museum's new food-service spaces.

The centrepiece of the remodelled museum is a five-storey atrium that provides glimpses of galleries all around and enables visitors to orient themselves as they wander from one area to another.

And Taniguchi went much further. He brought Philip Johnson's beloved sculpture garden back to its original size, changed the approach and restored the facade and staircase of Philip Goodwin and Edward Durell Stone's original 1939 MoMA, which was the first modern museum and one of the first International Style buildings in the US — built the same year as the Neoclassical National Gallery in Washington. (Saarinen Swanson and Saarinen had won a federal competition, also in 1939, for a geometric modern Smithsonian Art Gallery on the Washington Mall across from the National Gallery, but it was never built.)

The first new MoMA was a pristine little white marble-walled gem with banded windows, a curved canopy and a flat roof with cheese holes on a street of elaborate, traditional town houses and commercial buildings. It had thin, movable interior walls and intimate enclosed galleries. Only the members' room on the top floor, library, lobby and staircase were light-filled – at least until Johnson's walled garden elegantly opened up the urban site in 1953. His 1964 gallery wing on the west side of the original building lightened it further with black steel and glass walls framing gentle arches. These elements

have also been retained.

The despised escalators that were added along the garden wall during Pelli's 1977–84 renovation have been removed (or at least moved to a more discreet location in a hallway), but still move crowds smoothly. Working throughout with collaborating architects Kohn Pedersen Fox (KPF) of New York, engineers Guy Nordensen Associates and Severud Associates, Taniguchi also exposed the base of the gridded dark-glass apartment tower Pelli built, so that it can now be seen from the garden and is visibly, from both inside and outside the museum, part of the whole composition.

Most visitors pass the apartment tower as they approach the museum on West 53rd Street, as the main entrance has been moved down the block, which is now almost completely filled with MoMA buildings. The original facade has been converted to an entrance to the museum offices. Access to the new ground-floor restaurant, The Modern, which also occupies a privileged position along the long garden wall, is through Johnson's steel-and-glass addition.

The relocation of the main entrance means that most museum goers now not only have to walk further before

entering, but that, on entering, they do not immediately see much art. Instead, what they encounter are two long desks, a row of heavy columns, ribbons of elegant little halogen overhead lamps and another entrance across the block on 54th Street, as the lobby has become a public passage. Now, instead of walking by the busy book shop that used to open onto the lobby, and immediately being presented with sculpture in an exquisite outdoor setting, visitors enter a gigantic open concourse where tickets are sold, as they might be at an oversized theatre or for a plane to China. Even the cloakroom is hidden away to one side. The new book shop is tucked in behind a narrow entrance. Only those who enter from 54th Street can look up and into the museum itself right away, and they deserve something for trudging through the grim black-panelled and corrugated-steel facades here.

Art does not beckon most visitors until they are at least halfway through the passage, when they can look up and see glimpses of the galleries on the upper floors or turn 90 degrees and pass through the ticket-takers. The garden then comes into view, from its short end.

The pièce de résistance, however, is not visible until one climbs a flight of stairs and enters a gigantic atrium,

The original Museum of Modern Art, designed by Philip Goodwin and Edward Durell Stone in 1939, radically altered the largely residential block of West 53rd Street between Fifth and Sixth Avenues.

Today, most of West 53rd Street is given over to the museum, and a quiet Modernism rules. Philip Johnson's 1964 gallery wing, on the far right, now leads directly to The Modern restaurant. The original MoMA facade provides the entrance to the staff offices. Further west is Cesar Pelli's 1977–84 MoMA residential tower, with the new museum entrance and book shop beyond.

Close-up of the bold, curved canopy that sheltered the original 1939 museum and now leads to the staff offices upstairs. (above) Like most museums today, MoMA places emphasis on commercial space. The Bar Room, designed by Bentel & Bentel, with Danny Meyer and David Swinghamer of the Union Square Hospitality Group, provides glimpses into the museum. (top)

where Barnett Newman's enormous bronze Broken Obelisk, a group of Cy Twombly's paintings, and glimpses into surrounding galleries make this area, quite literally, stunning. Here, finally, you are in the world of art. Crowds buzz all around, yet there is a stillness.

Circulation is handled subtly, via multiple paths, views of the spaces beyond, and little arrows pointing to the galleries above the escalators. The collection is no longer shown in chronological order. Contemporary works are on the double-height first floor and visitors are taken back in time, upwards through increasingly intimate galleries, though the temporary exhibition galleries are right at the top. Instead of the old directed route, there are now choices, and more opportunity to wander. Being able to see from one gallery to the next means it is easy to choose a route and difficult to get lost.

There is little to detract from the works of art in the exquisitely detailed galleries with vents tucked into reveals.

The best part of the design is the way Taniguchi provides views, not only from one part of the museum to the next, but also outlooks onto the city, framing Manhattan towers, Art Moderne apartments, classical townhouses, steeples and vistas, so that looking at art has become part of the urban experience. In doing so, he brings art back to life.

MoMA at 65 has not ossified. It has simply grown up (and out). It never really was radical. It just seemed so when much of the US was contentedly isolated from the rest of the cultural world. The choices of the museum's curators were almost always informed and progressive in a mainstream way. The early work is largely European, since Europe led the avant-garde when it was done. The mid-

century collection reflects the rise of the New York School. And since Taniguchi was hired, Frank Gehry has not received a single museum commission (while the more self-effacing Renzo Piano has had half a dozen), and attention has turned to new museums by Herzog & de Meuron, Tadao Ando, Kazuyo Sejima & Ryue Nishizawa and Toyo Ito that share Taniguchi's subtle approach.

It is not yet clear whether multiple aesthetic directions will become the norm in the big wide globalised world. But more is being built in China than anywhere else, and while developers there are still looking westward, Yung Ho Chang (recently installed as chairman at MIT) and other members of the Chinese avant-garde are looking to Japan and Korea for inspiration. MoMA may still be ahead of the game. ⟁+

Dirk Cove

Niall McLaughlin Architects, Dirk Cove remodelled and extended former coastguard's cottage on the west coast of Ireland, 2004.

Jeremy Melvin describes how for Niall McLaughlin the remodelling of a coastguard's cottage, in a dramatic coastal setting in County Cork, offered a unique opportunity to render 'nature into ephemeral space'.

Whether its intricate and angular forms seem to mesh with the rocky shards of Ireland's west coast, or it appears as a focus for the light of a dawn halo, Niall Mclaughlin's remodelling of a coastguard's cottage engages in an interaction with its surroundings that is every bit as complex as the landscape and the traditions that have become interwoven with it. The jagged coastline evokes tortured relationships between the land's anguished history and the turbulent ocean, and the geological shapes give the bay the name Dirk (or Dagger) Cove. But there is also the possibility of catharsis which echoes what Seamus Heaney indicated in his poem 'Lovers on Aran':

> Did sea define the land or land
> the sea?
> Each drew new meaning from the
> waves' collision.
> Sea broke on land to full identity.

Appearing to evolve from the natural and artificial forms already on the site, and in its orientation towards the sea, McLaughlin's architecture explores these potential meanings.

The original purpose of the house had a strong bearing on its position, siting and construction, while its role as part of the machinery of British occupation in Ireland, albeit a small and relatively benign one, influenced its subsequent history. It lies at the end of the road: here land transport yielded to boats, and as those boats had to be launched in rough weather the location of the house and, in particular, the angle of the slipway take advantage of

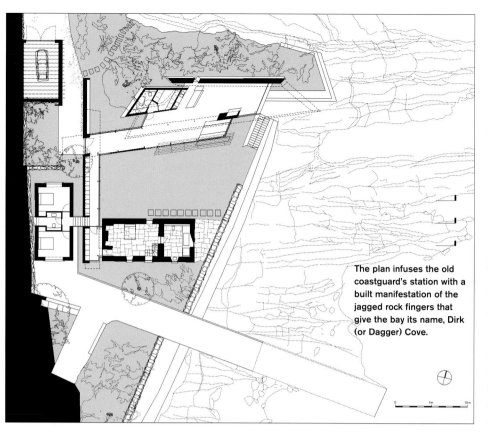

The plan infuses the old coastguard's station with a built manifestation of the jagged rock fingers that give the bay its name, Dirk (or Dagger) Cove.

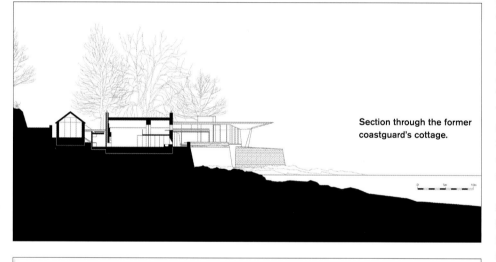

Section through the former coastguard's cottage.

Section through the courtyard.

the natural cove, which gives some protection from prevailing southwesterly storms.

The cottage itself, perhaps because its occupants had regularly to dice with death at sea, turns its back on the water, while its construction follows the vernacular convention of small windows and thick walls, so precluding easy connections between exterior and interior. But in the troubled period of the early 1920s, which saw the establishment of an independent Irish state, that mattered little. The coastguard's station fell into disrepair and, with resources for public services greatly stretched in the new and poverty-stricken country, it remained so, its brickwork and masonry gradually sinking into ruinous romance.

With social and economic progress, such picturesque attractions began to overcome the legacy of history. By the early 21st century, Ireland surpassed its former master in per capita affluence, and for the first time in centuries attracted immigrants from its diasporous communities. Under these circumstances, Dirk Cove, a dramatic and isolated site of great beauty, became an attractive proposition. Not far from Cork, it could be reached relatively easily by people living outside Ireland, but who wanted an accessible retreat. The challenge was to find an architecture that would draw out its inherent beauties without overwhelming its historic and natural significance.

McLaughlin is known for seductive and flamboyant forms, but certainly their seductiveness and perhaps their flamboyance are heightened by an extraordinary sensibility to the existing qualities of place. It might have been easy, in this landscape, to erase the traces of human occupation and start again in creating a direct relationship between nature and artifice. But instead Mclaughlin reused the old cottage, recognising that its construction, orientation and form had qualities that were appropriate for some of the activities in the new house. Consequently it was remodelled to provide a bedroom and bathroom suite, while its simple, orthogonal geometry helped to position the garage and entrance, and also suggested a discreet and protected

In a truly modern sense, the house offers a vantage point for contemplating nature (far left). From above the house is a constructed interpretation of the rocky shards (left). Its striking forms might suggest that the Irish coast inflects the orthogonal construction of Californian Case Study houses (below).

location for guest accommodation. McLaughlin describes the composition as a 'relatively lazy crucifix', and this easy relationship seems to have found a counterpart in a sympathetic county architect who was relaxed about the prospect of a contemporary building on this precious section of coast.

The homely, comforting building with its vernacular origins makes an appropriate sounding board for the most dramatic new element, the sharded and faceted living space. Visible from a distance, it disappears behind a thick wall that is parallel though staggered with the garage. Penetrating it through the entrance reveals each of the elements, but in a new relationship to each other. Ahead is the living space, a mass of light, shadow, frames, planes and cantilevers. To the right is the old cottage. And between the two is the closest such a site can have to a formal lawn, held in position by the sea wall. Beyond the living room, framed by the old and new buildings, is the ocean, uncontrollable, unfathomable, but rendered through a carefully contrived frame.

In this context, the powerful forms of the living area are fully appropriate. They might take their cue from the angular fingers of rock, dark and menacing, that penetrate the sea. If so, they mediate their elemental qualities into the finished materials of steel, glass and white render, while each angle and plane inflects the gaze towards a particular object or vista. This space turns the intense duel between land and sea into a delicate cat's cradle of light, reflection and shadow, turning and transforming into spatial qualities what nature left as purely volumetric.

Rendering nature into ephemeral space with an almost narrative-like ability to unfold over time merges with levels of comfort, such as the seats and fireplace, to make the room both congenial and stimulating. The sea can soothe or threaten, but here its dangers are turned into an aesthetic and emotional condition, recalling Ruskin's dictum that 'There is no such thing as bad weather, merely different types of good weather'. As if to prove the point, shortly after completion the house withstood the privations of a 100-year

storm with no noticeable damage, despite stones being thrown onto the lawn and seaweed onto the roof.

The house transforms McLaughlin's compositional 'lazy crucifix' into a symbolic one. Between the intimacy of a retreat and the openness that such a site invites is a powerful axis, while a weaker or more sinuous one runs across it, joining history and its traditions to conditions laid down by nature. It is the interaction between them that allows the restrictions of each pole to be transcended, to open the eyes to what lies beyond the limits of immediate perceptions, as Heaney hinted:

The timeless waves, bright sifting, broken glass
Came dazzling around, into the rocks,
Came glinting, sifting from the Americas. Δ+

Dirk Cove is also featured in Jeremy Melvin's forthcoming book, *Country Houses Today*, which will be published in the Interior Angles series by John Wiley & Sons in the spring of 2006.

Clarion Quay

A high-rise housing scheme in Dublin that disperses affordable units in the same blocks as privately owned apartments, Clarion Quay was planned as a key piece in the city's docklands regeneration. As **Robert Payne** describes, the architects, Urban Projects, chose to elevate the high-rise as a 'heroic' and 'expressive' form rather than turning their backs on the building type's Modernist past.

Urban Projects, Clarion Quay, Dublin, 2000
Looking down Excise Walk to the River Liffey is the social and affordable accommodation. Orientated north–south, the units face onto Mayor Square. The double-height winter garden access can be seen to the right.

Ireland's membership of the European Union, alongside a prosperous economy and a young population, has led to the reinvigoration of its major urban nodes, not least of which is the capital, Dublin. The city had, for many years, slowly declined and with this enthusiasm for renewal has come the opportunity to redevelop and regenerate several large brownfield sites in the heart of the urban fabric.

The Dublin Docklands Development Authority (DDDA) was founded in 1997 to regenerate 520 hectares (1285 acres) of land on the banks of the River Liffey between the centre of Dublin and the Irish Sea. This land had fallen into disuse following the introduction of containerised sea traffic, and the construction of new handling facilities closer to the mouth of the river. With the city centre nearby, and an extensive southern frontage to the river, the land presented an opportunity to evolve a type of urbanisation new to Dublin.

The proximity of areas of social deprivation, directly to the north of the development area, made the inclusion of social and affordable housing an essential part of the project from the outset. Earlier regeneration projects where the River Liffey passes through the city centre had proved less than successful because they neither addressed the need to create a diverse, and sustainable, social mix nor confronted the massing and scale issues demanded by the width of the river at this point.

The first master plan prepared by the DDDA sought to reverse this unsatisfactory pattern by proposing a mixed development, including housing, of which 20 per cent was to be designated as social and affordable. Quality of design was a fundamental parameter of the master plan and to achieve this, in 1998 the DDDA announced an architectural competition for a new public square and street connecting it to the river that would form the centrepiece of the regeneration project. The competition was won by Urban Projects, a consortium of like-minded architectural practices comprising Derek Tynan Architects, McGarry Ní Éanaigh Architects and Gerry Cahill Architects.

Although the winning scheme made proposals for both sides of the new public square and street, Urban Projects was appointed only to design its western half; the eastern half was passed to a number of corporate practices to be developed as a hotel and third-level college.

The final design closely follows the winning competition entry. It comprises two parts: a plinth surmounted by towers running along the new street, Excise Walk, between the River Liffey and the new public space, Mayor Square; and three slab blocks arranged around a garden courtyard that is open to the south. Unlike in the UK, there is next to no tradition of high-rise social housing in Ireland. Consequently, this form is not associated with failed ideals and economic deprivation in the same way as on Ireland's island neighbour. Indeed, it was seen as appropriate for the context of the site due to its location in the heart of the city and as a response to the width of the river it sits beside.

Two of the blocks are orientated east–west and contain units for sale. The third block faces north–south and houses the social and affordable units. To preserve a 19th-century remnant of the docklands architecture, which has been converted into a bar, the north–south block stands back from Mayor Street, the main circulation spine and shopping street of the regeneration zone. While it does not enjoy views of the river, this block occupies the prime position in the new garden courtyard where it faces south and contains a double-height ground-floor crèche, which opens into the courtyard. The architects were keen that this outside space would support mature trees. For this reason, it is founded on 'real ground': underground car parking is limited to the basements of the slab blocks.

The towers mentioned above rise to nine storeys, but are not described here, as they contain neither social nor affordable units. However, their heroic and innovative qualities extend to the design of the slab blocks as well. The north–south block, which contains the social and affordable housing, is seven storeys high, a scale appropriate to its riverside location.

From the start, both the DDDA and Urban Projects agreed that the social and affordable element of the scheme should be identical in form, spatial arrangement and materials to the units for sale. Of the 183 units eventually constructed, 37, or 20 per cent, were to be handed over on completion to be managed by a housing association selected through a tendering process. (The density of the scheme is 291 units per hectare, greatly in excess of the maximum density of 200 units per hectare prevailing in the city at the time.)

View into the newly created Excise Walk, looking up from the river. It includes retail space at ground level with residential accommodation above. Although the height of the development is unusual for Dublin, the location of the site, in the heart of the city and adjacent to the river, made it suitable for the programme.

In Ireland, social and affordable units are generally concentrated in stand-alone blocks rather than being dispersed through their host projects, to simplify management and minimise service charges. Looking at the inside first, there are five types of units, all of which enjoy a dual aspect, with bedrooms overlooking the main street to the north, and all living rooms facing the garden courtyard to the south. Nearly half of the units are two-storey, or 'duplex' units. The one-bedroom and duplex units have narrow frontages; the two- and three-bedroom single-storey units are wider, the former having single-aspect living rooms and the latter enjoying dual-aspect ones, running the full depth of the block. All living rooms have balconies behind the plane of the external walls to shelter them from the prevailing southwesterly wind, which is felt most acutely near the river.

At ground level, reasonably sized private terraces give onto the central courtyard. Above, balconies allow occupants of the remaining flats to enjoy the communal area.

To counter any association with the poor quality of deck access in previous social housing developments, high-standard materials and glazed weather screens have been used. The height of the access reflects the type of units the walkway serves – double-height for duplex apartments, single for one-storey apartments.

Floor-to-ceiling glazing and large sliding doors connect the inside and outside in a very direct way. The interiors of the units are finished to a high standard – identical to that provided in the units for sale. They include 'pod' bathrooms and kitchens, prefabricated in Italy, and hardwood windows and external doors. All of the units are wired for a range of electronic services, including cable television, which is universally provided in Dublin, and broadband.

Vertical circulation to the units is located in two cores, each containing a lift and stairs. Horizontal circulation is provided either directly from a lobby at each level or via two 'winter gardens' – external access decks that are partially shielded from the weather by glazing. Each winter garden is a short dead-end serving no more than five units. They are one or two storeys high, depending on whether they serve single-storey or duplex units. Both are paved with small concrete slabs and panelled in hardwood sheeting. The changes in height and the selection of finishes dispel any association with access decks commonly used in the city's stock of social apartments.

It is in the organisation of the scheme that the heroic aspects of the design – those associated with the precedents of international Modernism– are most evident, in the orientation of the living spaces towards the sun and the view of the garden, and in the adoption of a duplex section for nearly half of the units. The innovative aspects of the design can be found in its construction, in particular the use of prefabricated service elements – a new technology in Ireland when the building was constructed.

Outside, the heroic aspect of the design is more rhetorical. Here, there are streets in the air, floating planes, ribbon windows and a deployment of materials, such as brick, timber and glass, in forms that emphasise their roles as cladding rather than structure.

Internally, the quality of the materials specified reflects the care taken throughout the project. The apartments are orientated to face south wherever possible so as to maximise sun and daylight.

This rhetoric is well judged. Urban Projects must have been aware when designing a project in the very centre of the regeneration zone that it would be unable to exert control over adjoining plots that were yet to be developed. Equally, the architects must have been able to predict the sort of corporate architectural expression that was likely to follow.

They have therefore taken the norms of this corporate expression and reinvigorated it with the characteristics of early Modernism from which it derives, such as the streets in the air and the ribbon windows already mentioned. But they have gone a step further. They have combined the street in the air and the ribbon window to create a new kind of ambiguous indoor-–outdoor space: the winter garden. And then they have selected a yellow machine-made brick: crisp and modern, certainly, but also referring by means of its colour to the local stock 'grey' bricks of which the docklands were built.

Next, they have wrapped the top of the building in timber, detailing it not in the homely way of much current housing design, but in finely dimensioned strips, almost like metal cladding. Finally, there is the garden courtyard. Already, after only a few years of occupation, this feels like a 'place', justifying the determination of the architects to make the garden on real ground.

On their completion in 2000, the social and affordable units were allocated to candidates on the housing waiting list of the local authority, Dublin City Council, in accordance with established procedures. Unusually, Cluid Housing Association, a branch of the St Pancras Housing Association, which manages the block, was not involved in the design process. The perceived luxury of the development, the generous space standards that exceed norms for social and affordable housing by 20 per cent, and the involvement of the tenants in the maintenance to encourage participation and reduce service charges, have all helped to forge a settled and contented community. After a number of years of occupation it is evident that the simplicity of the design and the robustness of the construction have contributed to this, not least by making maintenance easy.

While it may be a pioneering project, Clarion Quay is not a hesitant one. The directness of its external expression establishes a scale and massing appropriate to the width of the river, in critical contrast to the earlier developments upstream: its assured space-making means that both the garden courtyard at ground level and the winter gardens as culs-de-sac in the air have made clear from the start how they are to be used and where the boundaries lie between public and private space. And the ingenuity of the internal planning has given all occupants, both owners and tenants, a sense of generosity and privacy, paradoxically within the framework of increased density.

Clarion Quay exhibits a confidence that raises the spirit of anyone who visits the project, whether professional or layperson, and points clearly to the future direction of social and affordable housing in the context of urban regeneration in Ireland. ᗑ+

Robert Payne studied at University College Dublin from 1977 to 1982. Having worked with Arup Associates and Allies and Morrison in London, he founded Cullen Payne Architects with Brian Cullen in 1994, winning an international competition for the Institute of Material Sciences at Trinity College the following year. He teaches at a number of schools of architecture and contributes to journals both in the UK and abroad.

CLARION QUAY	G 0-29%	F 30-39%	E 40%	D 41-49%	C 50-59%	B 60-69%	A 70-100%
QUALITATIVE							
Space-Interior							A
Space-Exterior							A
Location							A
Community							A
QUANTITATIVE							
Construction Cost							unknown
Cost-rental/purchase							unknown
Cost in use							unknown
Sustainability							unknown
AESTHETICS							
Good Design?							A
Appeal							A
Innovative?							A

This table is based on an analytical method of success in contributing to a solution to housing need. The criteria are: Quality of life – does the project maintain or improve good basic standards? Quantitative factors – has the budget achieved the best it can? Aesthetics – does the building work visually?

Metrogramma

Metrogramma with Foreign Office Architects (FOA) and Luca Molinari, competition entry (third place) for Lombardy Region new head office, Milan, 2004.

Luigi Prestinenza Puglisi describes how the two principals of Metrogramma, an emerging office in Milan, drew on their postgraduate experiences in New York and the Netherlands to inform the dynamic manner in which they practise. Building up their practice through strategic urban planning, they are now setting their sights on major architectural schemes.

In 1995, Andrea Boschetti and Alberto Francini, graduates of Venice and Florence universities, two of the most traditionalist establishments, hermetically sealed to innovation and experimentation, did the right thing. Andrea Boschetti went to Columbia University in America and then to Rotterdam in the Netherlands, where he worked for Rem Koolhaas, a theorist of the contemporary metropolis and an architect then emerging within the international scene with his completion of Euralille and several other masterpieces. Alberto Francini went first to New York to work in the practice of Giuliano Fiorenzuoli, a leading figure in the radical Florentine architecture of the 1960s and 1970s, and then to Rome, where he worked with Massimiliano Fuksas, who was also at the time rapidly rising to fame.

Like many other young Italian architects of their generation, Boschetti and Francini realised that it was necessary to radically question many of the dogmas that continue to dominate the conservative culture of a country still marked by the rigorism of Vittorio Gregotti, by the historicism of Aldo Rossi and by the Postmodernism of Paolo Portoghesi. It was necessary to open up to the reasoning of the avant-garde, albeit revised by the demands of the market, as taught by Koolhaas and Fuksas with much realism or, if you like, a certain cynicism.

Metrogramma was set up in Milan in 1998 – a year after the Guggenheim Museum opened in Bilbao and two years before the successful Venice Architecture Biennale directed by Fuksas. These two events marked the architectonic debate in Italy, liberating youthful energies and resulting in a radical change of perspective.

The Guggenheim, with its immense international success, showed the concrete possibility of breaking new ground in formal research that went beyond the simplified geometries and the rigour of the right-angle so beloved by traditionalists. And the Venice Architecture Biennale, with its provocative subtitle 'More Ethics, Less Aesthetics', suggested the contemporary city as a complex and chaotic whole, rizomatic and contradictory. The city could no longer be reduced to the simplistic and authoritarian urban design models – those academic exercises based on axes, alignments and symmetries and, in the best examples, on an analysis of building types and the morphology of the space – that at the time were still being taught in Italian faculties of architecture.

At this point, many young practices were emerging onto the national scene, and Metrogramma found it had conceptual affinities and common interests with some of them. In 2000, the *5tudi* (an abbreviation of '5 practices') book series published a collection of works by Metrogramma alongside those by Privilegio-Secchi, Mantia, IaN+ and Stalker. It also introduced Bart Lootsma and Yorgos Simeoforidis, two of the international critics most interested in novelty and experimentation.

Simeoforidis began his contribution thus: 'There is certainly something moving in contemporary Italian architecture. The signs are there to see: young architects are distinguishing themselves in both national and international competitions, organising travelling exhibitions, participating in joint ventures and opening innovative breaches in university curricula. They are promoting their work themselves, without waiting for attention from the cultural establishment … They are architects that transcend the introversion of Italian architecture, and declare an open and flexible disposition.'

Although Metrogramma joined the scene at the right time, in the midst of the renewal of the architectonic culture in Italy, the practice immediately faced two obstacles. First, to many members of the public, the word 'building' is almost synonymous with 'crime' when it comes to decisively modern developments in nonperipheral areas, evoking the nightmare of speculation, of profiting from the sweat of the masses, and of environmental neglect. Second, the few projects that were still available at the time were monopolised by a restricted circle of professionals who exercised strict control over the territory – a situation that though now much better, is still far from satisfactory. Through complex alchemies, such control even extended to architecture competitions with 'select' juries.

If work is scarce, it is necessary to invent some, and to do so Metrogramma took its inspiration from the Dutch way, which seeks to show that creativity, traditionally characteristic of the architect, does not serve only to produce objects that are aesthetically pleasing, but can preconfigure better spatial planning, producing added value both financially and in terms of improved quality of life. Thus, 'building' does not mean pouring in more cement and degrading the land, as environmentalist and conservationists too often believe. It means enabling a different conformation of metropolitan relations to find new ways of using space, new ecologies, new conventions and new opportunities.

With this programme of work, the practice gained the attention of the mayor of Bolzano, Silvano Bassetti, an enlightened administrator. This collaboration resulted in a report, *Habitat* (2001), which envisaged dividing the efficient and well-governed city of Bolzano into four macro-zones: the agrocity, or agricultural area; the policity, or the area related to the mountain; the 'cityn', or the consolidated area; and the border city, or the outskirts.

For each of these, rigid spaces were set aside for the community, and flexible zones were destined for private building. However, this was all on the understanding that developments must improve, and not worsen, the current situation. For example, buildings were to include energy-saving devices, which led to the invention of the energy-efficient house and 'green roofs',

methods of increasing transpiration from the ground and using energy supplied from the roofing too.

In its next report, *Superinfrastructures* (2003), on behalf of the National Confederation of Tradesmen (CNA), Metrogramma maintain that the ground should not be covered by thousands of industrial buildings sitting indiscriminately, cheek by jowl, like the houses in a demented suburban sprawl. Instead, they posit three new types of building – tower settlements, ribbon settlements and slab settlements – that allow the community to save land, and individuals to cut costs. Here, Metrogramma reuse point, line and surface, taking from a famous affirmation by the painter Kandinsky, which Bernard Tschumi (dean Columbia's School of Architecture) later appropriated for one of his famous projects, the Parc de la Villette in Paris.

The report also makes reference to Koolhaas's idea of 'bigness', of building a complex settlement, almost a macro-structure, that straddles mere architecture and town planning. However, Metrogramma's proposal is more attractive. 'Mixitè', to use their term, involves putting several functions alongside each other. Industrial buildings, as well as being imposing, co-owned structures, should include shops, restaurants, leisure facilities and homes. The need for such schemes is particularly acute in the north of Italy, where demand for affordable houses and facilities is high to meet the requirements of immigrants, especially from outside the EU, who are employed in these production facilities.

The practice's proposal for the new library in Guadalajara, Mexico, returns to the idea of bigness, and is perhaps one of Metrogramma's most interesting projects. It is a gigantic sphere about 70 metres (230 feet) in diameter, the result of a desire to create a monument of absolute geometric purity that would almost clash with the surrounding city, and which recalls the visionary architecture of French architect Claude-

Nicolas Ledoux (1736–1806). However, there are also functional motivations: the sphere is the geometric shape that encloses the greatest volume in the smallest surface area and, conceptually speaking, is therefore the most economical shape to house the collection of millions of books in the library's care.

In contrast to the stereometric purity of the exterior, the library interior – like the work of the Italian sculptor Arnaldo Pomodoro – is extremely complex and jagged. The reading rooms, auditorium, meeting rooms and vertical and horizontal pathways are obtained by excavating a continuum of galleries and spaces from the mass of the building, arranged without any apparent order, following the same reductive logic as Koolhaas used for his National Library of France project in 1989. In Metrogramma's project, the interior labyrinth of pathways and holes, reminiscent of a termite mound or a Swiss cheese, formed a counterpoint to the pure prism of the exterior. Simplicity and complexity, order and chaos, a monumental exterior and an anti-monumental interior, but above all experimentation with new typologies that are attractive from the functional point of view, and that allow experimentation on the wall of the shape. But a shape conceived from the plans, from the theme's adherence to the social, economic and ecological conditions of the context and which thus produces a surplus value that can be plainly measured against the ever more demanding and complex parameters of postindustrial society.

See, for example, Metrogramma's Descho showroom in south Bolzano, which is built inside an industrial building and located on the first floor to leave the ground floor for goods deliveries. For a shop, this would be a terrible location, separated from the street and from the passing trade, but here form comes to the rescue thanks to a curve linking the showroom to the floor above, framed in turn by a large window. The result is a winning and innovative picture, but also one that perfectly fits the client's requirements, following the Dutch example.

As for integrating different functions, the practice's Calliano complex (completed in 2002 and nominated for the 2002 Mies van der Rohe prize) combines a nursery, secondary school, library, gymnasium, canteen and a cultural centre in a single building of unusual style. The different functions within the building are underlined by the use of different materials, while careful planning of pathways achieves unity of the spatial concept. This follows a long tradition stretching from Le Corbusier's architectural promenade to Koolhaas's use of the architectonic continuum.

Again experimenting with different styles is Metrogramma's competition entry for the Lombardy region new head office, designed in partnership with Foreign Office Architects (FOA) and Luca Molinari. This was a very tempting project that was put out to tender in 2004, and many of the world's leading design practices measured themselves against it. The idea was to build a skyscraper in three parts, which would join up on the upper floors, thus leaving space on the ground for a covered piazza. Moreover, on the top floor, more than 100 metres (328 feet) up, a space was to be provided for social and cultural functions, giving a panoramic view over the whole of Milan.

Metrogramma's entry came third, beating competitors such as Norman Foster and Steven Holl – not bad for a team that had only been formed a few years earlier and now, thanks to its work promoting new ideas, has five or six prestigious commissions on the drawing board. These include a pharmaceutical centre in Barcelona and a number of villa housing developments in Bolzano, comprising around 40 homes – a sign that even in traditionalist Italy, experimentation, if done with enough intellectual energy and sufficient self-promotion, can win through. ∆+

Luigi Prestinenza Puglisi is an architecture critic, and teaches history of contemporary architecture at the University of Rome. His books include *HyperArchitecture* (Birkhauser, 1999). He writes for *Domus*, *Abitare*, *L'Arca*, *A10*, *Monument* and *The Architects' Newspaper*. See www.prestinenza.it.

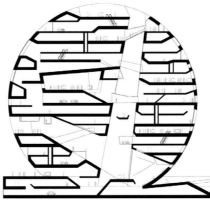

Metrogramma, competition entry for Guadalajara Library, Guadalajara, Mexico, 2005
This project recalls both the visionary architecture of the French architect Claude-Nicolas Ledoux and Rem Koolhaas's concept of 'bigness'.

Metrogramma, services centre and school building with multifunctional spaces, Calliano, Bolzano, Italy, 2002
This complex combines a school building (comprising a nursery and a secondary school) with multifunctional spaces open to the community, such as a library, gymnasium, canteen and a cultural centre, in a single building. The development occupies an area of 4500 square metres (48,438 square feet) with an 800-square-metre (8610-square-foot) extension making a total volume of 5000 cubic metres (176,573 cubic feet). The building overlooks the banks of the River Adige, the Brenner motorway and the railway. Like a cruise ship, inside it houses functional programmes that are contiguous and heterogeneous both for the time and uses – teaching, cultural, sporting and recreational.

Metrogramma, Superinfrastructures: Consortium 10, manufacturing condominium, former Iveco site, Bolzano, Italy, due for completion 2007
The project was a result of the *Superinfrastructures* study the practice carried out for the National Confederation of Tradesmen (CNA) to rationalise land use and avoid the proliferation of isolated industrial buildings that blot the landscape indiscriminately, side by side. 'Mixitè' involves placing several functions alongside each other. The building is actually a manufacturing condominium covering 10,500 square metres (113,000 square feet), which is 20 metres (66 feet) high and houses 16 different businesses offering various services. Warehouses are planned in the basement, workshops and exhibition spaces on the first and second floors, and offices on the third floor. The fourth floor will house offices and homes related to the activities downstairs. The building is situated on an angular site, in a block, where a further two similar buildings are planned. It therefore has two blind sides on the contiguous sites (north and west) and two open sides exposed to the light.

Metrogramma with Foreign Office Architects (FOA) and Luca Molinari, competition entry (third place) for Lombardy region new head office, Milan, 2004
In this project, Metrogramma and FOA have tried to imagine a contemporary monument for Milan and Lombardy.

They state their intentions as: 'At once an unparalleled symbol and a space generated by the city; a space that is a civic piazza and a work space at the same time, a symbol of the landscape and the urban infrastructure.'

The social and contemplative spaces are at a height of 100 metres (328 feet), making the most of the panoramic view over the landscape, while on the ground the building is closely interrelated with the city, from the Garibaldi campus to the public transport network. The building's auditorium and entrance hall are sunken into a green space that functions as a public park.

**Metrogramma, Farmhispania Laboratory
Building, Barcelona, Spain, 2006**
This building plays on the chiaroscuro effects of
the aluminium sheets covering the facade.

Resumé

1998
Andrea Boschetti and Alberto Francini found
Metrogramma

Invited competition for three industrial sheds
in Bolzano: first place

1999
Competition for Sarajevo concert hall:
special mention

2000
Project of a plant at 7th International
Architecture Fair 'Futuramay2k', Venice

Gruber Center trading building and offices,
Bolzano: due for completion 2008

2001
Descho showroom and annexed storehouse,
Bolzano: nominated for Mies van der Rohe
prize, 2002

2002
Multifunctional building in Calliano, Bolzano:
nominated for Mies van der Rohe prize, 2002

RSA 'Solatrix due' nursing home, Rovereto:
due for completion 2008

2003
*Superinfrastructure: insediamenti produttivi
ad alta densità* (Superinfrastructures:
high-density productive settlements)

Feasibility planning and construction of Villa
Giardino maso della Pieve residential
building, Bolzano: due for completion 2006

Final planning and construction of Domus
Malles residential building, Bolzano: due for
completion 2006

Manufacturing condominium, former Iveco
site, Bolzano: due for completion 2007

2004
International competition for new
headquarters for the Lombardy region:
third place

2005
Competition entry for Guadalajara Library,
Guadalajara, Mexico

2006
Farmhispania Laboratory Building, Barcelona

McLean's Nuggets

Bruce and William McLean with North Ayrshire Council, Dalry Primary School – Model 1, 2001.

What Does Learning Look Like?

When architects do their job and take seriously the role of social servant they must ceaselessly ask questions of the work they have been invited to undertake or have appropriately invented, especially in the case of the design and unnecessary recognition of the building type, such as that of a school. Current primary-school design in the UK is predicated on a year system, a corresponding floor area per child, per class (of 1.49 square metres) and the accumulated government debris of the national curriculum. An unquestioning acceptance of the brief and, thus, the purpose of such projects leave only the act or alleged 'art' of design to transcend the prosaic. What does learning look like? And how might your physical environment be a useful employable or deployable tool for its experience? One answer is that your constructed physical environment may be no use at all. Architect Aldo van Eyck's childhood school in Hampstead, or Kilquhanity school in Scotland set up by AS Neil friend and like-minded pedagogue John Aitkenhead, were still fabricated environments, but their physical presence was an annotated landscape, with trees marked as meeting points and furniture something you are prepared to

carry. This educational land-use evokes Cedric Price's Potteries Thinkbelt project: a 100-square-mile (260-square-kilometre), 24-hour living toy of learning for 20,000 students in the derelict industrial zone of North Staffordshire, unfortunately in the 'sidings' for 30 years. Do new educational or learning models need to get lighter? One lightweight educational model is Klaas Hoek and Corrina Till's Slade Breakfast Club, an early morning mental exercise around a 3.6-metre (12-foot) diameter circular table, with tea, coffee and invited guests, with the quality of the ad-hoc servicing, part of what Professor Bruce McLean (Slade School of Art, UCL) describes as the 'lunching, learning and laughing theory of practical intelligence'. Professor Sir Graham Hills, speaking recently at the Royal Society of Arts (RSA), said that the teaching of explicit knowledge in the age of the World Wide Web is an anomaly and that 'the real purpose of education is to acquire as little knowledge as possible commensurate with your being capable, intelligent and of course, wise'. The title of his lecture, 'Knowledge is luggage: travel light'. So what, in these circumstances, is the purpose of an educational establishment? Ivan D Illich had no doubt that the knowledge industry had long since forgotten its intended purpose: 'The right to learn is curtailed by the obligation to attend school'. In his 1970 book *Deschooling Society*, Illich systematically dismantles the half-baked pseudo-specialism of education and educational tools as expensive and second-rate instruments of unhappy pedagogic orthodoxies, and presciently talks of learning webs as the key to a more diverse acceptance of where and when and how we learn. So what is the physical presence of the new

school and its key determinants? Buckminster Fuller believed (perhaps as a result of his transcendentalist family upbringing) that mind and body activities such as sports, music and dance created an 'intuitive dynamic sense', so if we are to avoid enforced physical exercise regimes, which sound about as much fun as organised fun, then distance, action and place might be useful factors in the conception of any learning system: moving, change of scene imperatives (not obligations) that stimulate and refresh one's appetite for mental stimulation. The Invisible University established by Samantha Hardingham, David Greene, John Frazer, Dr Victoria Watson et al is predicated on lightweight delivery systems and forums, and an acknowledgement of social function. Its key structural components are timetables and a self-appointed caretaker. Originating from David Greene's L.A.W.U.N. project of 1970, the possibilities of a geographically mobile learning network are re-examined without the acknowledged qualifications product of Harold Wilson's useful legacy: the Open University. So what other learning projects are in the making? In Russia, Natalia Vodianova's Naked Heart Foundation plans to deliver 200 Adam Kalkin-designed playhouses, positioned in public squares across the country. These shipping-container agglomerations are the new local 'light' industry. And, finally, a collaborative project between North Ayrshire Technical Services, Bruce McLean and myself sees the deployment of what has been described as 'embedded intelligence' in the form of text, symbol, code, number and puzzle physically embodied within the fabric and geometry of a new primary school in Dalry, due to open this autumn.

It's a Wrap

One industry that continues to technologically develop and diversify is the packaging industry. Never mind the product, just look at the packaging or, in some cases, taste the packaging. While the nutritional content of the tapioca-starch 'plastic' bags of the supermarket might not be highly rated, they can fully biodegrade in 8 to 12 weeks. Or what about the maize-starch plastic film for wrapping food or the rediscovery of cellophane – an early polymeric material invented in 1892 and yet another starch-based 100 per cent biodegradable product? The impetus for technological change does not only relate to packaging disposal, although packaging accounts for upwards of 30 per cent of all solid waste by weight (according to the Environmental Protection Agency in the US). What about packaging's structural qualities? Architect Shigeru Ban has clearly exploited the helically wound cardboard tube, but what about the developed surfaces of Pepin Press's *How to Fold*? Other advances include so-called intelligent inks: thermochromic for colour change, which we already see on bottles of Newcastle Brown Ale and KitKat chocolate bars, indicating optimum temperature for consumption; and other indicative inks acting as 'ripeness' sensors or showing bacterial content and shelf life. Add to this an optimised, robotic assembly line by KUKU Robotics Corporation and you have a construction industry of containers, albeit at a different scale.

What About Learning, Again?

According to a recent report in the *Observer* newspaper, Krister Svensson, director of the Stockholm International Toy Research Centre (SITEC) has explained that many, if not all, 'educational' toys are nothing of the sort. Too prescriptive, limited by their makers' imaginations and pedagogic dogma. Unsurprisingly, the research highlights the educational, or *learning*, advantage to be gained through the more ubiquitous and economic technology of the cardboard box. So what, if anything, do toys have to offer the imaginative potential of children? Freidrich Froebel (the originator of the term *Kindergarten*) conceived of and produced a range of Froebel building blocks, or 'gifts' as he described them, for the spatial and visual development of children. Simon Beeson of Edinburgh College of Art has recently initialised a project entitled Block City, which involves artists, architects and teachers speculating on future derivations/iterations of these learning instruments. Sir Harry Kroto, the Nobel Prize-winning chemist credited with the co-discovery of the C60 carbon molecule (Buckminster Fullerene) correlates the 'dearth of engineers and scientists in the West fairly and squarely on the fact that Lego has replaced Meccano (Erector Sets) as a toy of choice in many homes'. Kroto attacks Lego's fixed modularity as too limited a palette to usefully explore the intuitive engineering of a child. Seymour Papert (MIT) developed the Lego/Logo programmable brick system, which is commercially available as Lego Mindstorms, as an attempt to expand the range of the Danish toy as a modelling tool. A microprocessor (RCX Microcomputer) and a range of proprietary and custom analogues to digital sensors, with simple software, have become a prototypical robotic development tool, which still includes the recognisable push-fit Lego dimples. A very similar conception of embedded processing was John and Julia Frazer's

machine-readable models of 1980, which include Intelligent Beermats – reconfigurable beer-mat sized circuit boards for spatial experimentation on the back of the proverbial. New digital toys also offer a renewed interest in the physical to digital interface. Nintendo's Yoshi Topsy-Turvy and Wario Ware: Twisted for Game Boy Advance employ tilt switches within the game cartridge to acknowledge a more physical contribution to the playing of games as opposed to the rapid pressing of buttons. The use of simple sensors within this type of game suggests many possibilities where the temperature, light conditions or loudness of your environment could directly affect the outcome of a game. Another excellent digital 'toy' is Sodaplay's Sodaconstructor (www.sodaplay.com) where gravity and kinetic motion determine the actions of your digital drawings, which seems so much more enjoyable than any number of CAD programs. *D+*

'McLean's Nuggets' is an ongoing technical series inspired by Will McLean and Samantha Hardingham's enthusiasm for back issues of *D*, as explicitly explored in Hardingham's *D* issue *The 1970s is Here and Now* (March/April 2005). Will McLean is joint coordinator of technical studies in the Department of Architecture at the University of Westminster with Pete Silver. Together they have recently completed a new book entitled *Fabrication: The Designer's Guide* (Elsevier, 2006).

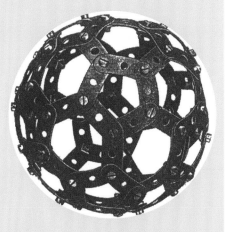

Page from *Meccano Magazine*, 1928, reproduced in Sir Harry Kroto's contribution to *Buckminster Fuller: An Anthology for a New Millennium*, edited by Thomas TK Zung.

Australian Wildlife Health Centre, Healesville Sanctuary, Melbourne

Leon van Schaik places Minifie Nixon's experimental Australian Wildlife Health Centre at Healesville Sanctuary, just outside Melbourne, within the wider context of the city's architectural culture.

View from Federation Square of the western horizon of Melbourne across Flinders Street station.

Melbourne has just been declared – yet again – one of the world's most liveable cities, just behind Vancouver this time. It has been just ahead before. A friend back from five months in Istanbul is revelling in the ease with which he can get about here, even as he shows me photograph after photograph of limpid air over the Bosphorus, and pictures of his family dining under mulberry trees in their back yard on one of Istanbul's many hills. The conversation became a little tiresome, he remarks – all art and politics and no sport! Somehow this vignette says a lot to me about the business of being liveable.

I want to argue that Melbourne is much more than that: that there is art and architecture, as well as sport. Politics would be pushing it a bit too far, I acknowledge, when both major political parties are playing to the gallery, exploiting fear, and content with the most minimal of investments in our intellectual development. Something there is in this city that drives an urge to be architecturally inventive, despite the odds. And curiously there is a role for sport in this – in the coffee bars people talk of their peers in sporting terms: so and so is an architect in the league of Schumacher or Federer. Of course they are ambitious and demanding! It is only natural.

But there is something else at work in the geopolitics of this city, with its hugely mixed population, 40 per cent of whom were born in some country other than Australia. It lies in the development processes that underpin the urban economy. About 80,000 houses are built here every year, 60 per cent of them on the urban fringe, many of these in the regional hinterland. It is in 3 per cent of these houses and in the crèches and health centres built to service them that much of the architectural invention of the city originates. Where everything is new, anything can be tried.

Minifie Nixon is conducting its latest architectural experiment, the Australian Wildlife Health Centre, at Healesville Sanctuary in the foothills of the Great Dividing Range, an hour and a half's drive to the east of the city. This is a hospital for wild animals, marking the return – as also with the Cassandra Complex Platypusary that is on the cover of *Design City Melbourne* (a 2006 title in the Wiley-Academy's Interior Angles series) – of Melbourne Zoo to the commissioning of innovative architects.

The exterior of the wildlife centre is composed of two different concrete blocks organised in a pattern generated in a cellular automata process. The innermost space is a 'costa' surface, a surface that is the smallest area it can be without intersecting itself, given its constraints. A helix and a paraboloid are such surfaces. This one serves as a contemporary form of the dome, lit by skylights, giving to visitors a sense that they are outside while in fact they are inside – aligning with the basic concept of the sanctuary – and that they are observing animals in their natural habitat. Importantly the central space is coloured gold, to distance it from the pure-white formal explorations of sculptors like Jean Arp and from the self-coloured fabric structures of lightweight-structure designers.

What *Design City Melbourne* shows is how works such as this relate to commissions won on the civic spine of the city, where the inventions become part of the popular imaginary of the city, contributing to an ongoing argument about its nature. Minifie Nixon has already built on the spine – the Centre for Ideas at the Victorian College for the Arts, a building that appeared on the cover of *Mastering Architecture: Becoming a Creative Innovator in Practice* (Wiley-Academy, 2005).

The design for the Centre for Ideas is formed by locating a series of Voronoi cells (polygonal sections generated from cones, the sections' ridges defining the points at which the surface is closer to

Render of entrance elevation. View showing the 'Costa' central space (top).
Entrance elevation under construction (bottom).

The paradoxical inside-outside space around the costa surface.

The view to the apex of the dome is remarkably similar to the view to the lantern in the centre of Burley Griffin and Marian Mahoney's dome at Newman College.

Play rages between centre and periphery, and there is no 'off-side' rule. So, too, in architecture in this city, the connoisseurs understand when an architect is passing forward in front of the line of play in order to create 'new options'. This is the name of our game.

another cone) over oculi located on the face of the building relative to internal needs, at which there are openings into the new spaces extended behind the new skin. This skin, in embossed stainless steel, may be cool in conception, but it captures the sky in reflection all day long, steely grey in some lights, ashen blue in others, and glowing gold in red sunsets. The Australian Wildlife Health Centre is a postscript to this building, which in its turn flowed from work exhibited at the Archilab exhibition in Orleans, 'Futurehouse', in 2001,[1] where they exhibited Orleans Batwing, a mathematically derived complex surface, both structure and wall, which served as a support for apartments.

So to the sporting intelligence there is much that is familiar in this movement between centre and periphery, between experimental fringe and declarative centre. And to a sporting intelligence, the managing of your career through carefully considered moves between these

different 'leagues' is second nature. Melbourne is the home of Australian rules football, an extraordinary game involving improbably large numbers of players on a cricket field oval and involving astronomical scores, by soccer standards anyway. Play rages between centre and periphery, and there is no 'off-side' rule. So, too, in architecture in this city, the connoisseurs understand when an architect is passing forward in front of the line of play in order to create 'new options'. This is the name of our game. ᴆ+

Note
1. In Marie-Ange Brayer and Beatrice Simonot (eds), *Archilab's Futurehouse: Radical Experiments in Living Space,* Thames & Hudson (London), 2001.

Leon van Schaik AO is Innovation Professor of Architecture at RMIT, Melbourne. At RMIT, he has developed a unique practice-based research programme for architects and designers. He is the author of *Mastering Architecture: Becoming a Creative Innovator in Practice* (2005) and *Design City Melbourne* (2006), both published on the Wiley-Academy architecture list by John Wiley & Sons.

△ **Architectural Design Magazine**

Subscription

As an influential and prestigious architectural publication, *Architectural Design* has an almost unrivalled reputation worldwide. Published bimonthly, it successfully combines the currency and topicality of a newsstand journal with the editorial rigour and design qualities of a book. Consistently at the forefront of cultural thought and design since the 1960s, it has time and again proved provocative and inspirational – inspiring theoretical, creative and technological advances. Prominent in the 1980s for the part it played in Postmodernism and then in Deconstruction, △ also took a pioneering role in the technological revolution of the 1990s. With groundbreaking titles dealing with cyberspace and hypersurface architecture, it has pursued the conceptual and critical implications of high-end computer software and virtual realities. △

SUBSCRIPTION RATES 2006
Institutional Rate (Print only or Online only): UK£175/US$290
Institutional Rate (Combined Print and Online): UK£193/US£320
Personal Rate (Print only): UK £99/US$155
Discount Student* Rate (Print only): UK£70/US$110

*Proof of studentship will be required when placing an order. Prices reflect rates for a 2006 subscription and are subject to change without notice.

TO SUBSCRIBE
Phone your credit card order:
+44 (0)1243 843 828

Fax your credit card order to:
+44 (0)1243 770 432

Email your credit card order to:
cs-journals@wiley.co.uk

Post your credit card or cheque order to:
John Wiley & Sons Ltd.
Journals Administration Department
1 Oldlands Way
Bognor Regis
West Sussex PO22 9SA
UK

Please include your postal delivery address with your order.

All △ volumes are available individually. To place an order please write to:
John Wiley & Sons Ltd
Customer Services
1 Oldlands Way
Bognor Regis
West Sussex PO22 9SA

Please quote the ISBN number of the issue(s) you are ordering.

△ is available to purchase on both a subscription basis and as individual volumes

○ I wish to subscribe to △ *Architectural Design* at the **Institutional rate of (Print only or Online only** *(delete as applicable)* £175/US$290.

○ I wish to subscribe to △ *Architectural Design* at the **Institutional rate of (Combined Print and Online) £193/US$320.**

○ I wish to subscribe to △ *Architectural Design* at the **Personal rate of £99/US$155.**

○ I wish to subscribe to △ *Architectural Design* at the **Student rate of £70/US$110.**

○ △ *Architectural Design* is available to individuals on either a calendar year or rolling annual basis; Institutional subscriptions are only available on a calendar year basis. Tick this box if you would like your Personal or Student subscription on a rolling annual basis.

Payment enclosed by Cheque/Money order/Drafts.
Value/Currency £/US$ ▭

○ Please charge £/US$ ▭ to my credit card.
Account number:
▭▭▭▭▭▭▭▭▭▭▭▭▭▭▭▭

Expiry date:
▭▭▭▭▭

Card: Visa/Amex/Mastercard/Eurocard *(delete as applicable)*

Cardholder's signature ▭
Cardholder's name ▭
Address ▭
▭
Post/Zip Code ▭

Recipient's name ▭
Address ▭
▭
Post/Zip Code ▭

I would like to buy the following issues:

○ △ 180 *Techniques and Technologies in Morphogenetic Design,* Michael Hensel, Achim Menges + Michael Weinstock

○ △ 179 *Manmade Modular Megastructures,* Ian Abley + Jonathan Schwinge

○ △ 178 *Sensing the 21st-Century City,* Brian McGrath + Grahame Shane

○ △ 177 *The New Mix,* Sara Caples and Everardo Jefferson

○ △ 176 *Design Through Making,* Bob Sheil

○ △ 175 *Food + The City,* Karen A Franck

○ △ 174 *The 1970s Is Here and Now,* Samantha Hardingham

○ △ 173 *4dspace: Interactive Architecture,* Lucy Bullivant

○ △ 172 *Islam + Architecture,* Sabiha Foster

○ △ 171 *Back To School,* Michael Chadwick

○ △ 170 *The Challenge of Suburbia,* Ilka + Andreas Ruby

○ △ 169 *Emergence,* Michael Hensel, Achim Menges + Michael Weinstock

○ △ 168 *Extreme Sites,* Deborah Gans + Claire Weisz

○ △ 167 *Property Development,* David Sokol

○ △ 166 *Club Culture,* Eleanor Curtis

○ △ 165 *Urban Flashes Asia,* Nicholas Boyarsky + Peter Lang

○ △ 164 *Home Front: New Developments in Housing,* Lucy Bullivant

○ △ 163 *Art + Architecture,* Ivan Margolius

○ △ 162 *Surface Consciousness,* Mark Taylor

○ △ 161 *Off the Radar,* Brian Carter + Annette LeCuyer

○ △ 160 *Food + Architecture,* Karen A Franck

○ △ 159 *Versioning in Architecture,* SHoP

○ △ 158 *Furniture + Architecture,* Edwin Heathcote

○ △ 157 *Reflexive Architecture,* Neil Spiller

○ △ 156 *Poetics in Architecture,* Leon van Schaik